THE PLAYWRIGHTS' CENTER MONOLOGUES FOR MEN

THE PLAYWRIGHTS' CENTER MONOLOGUES

FOR

MEN

EDITED BY KRISTEN GANDROW
AND POLLY K. CARL

HEINEMANN
Portsmouth, NH

Heinemann
A division of Reed Elsevier Inc.
361 Hanover Street
Portsmouth, NH 03801–3912
www.heinemanndrama.com

Offices and agents throughout the world

Performance rights information can be found on pages 153–54.

Library of Congress Cataloging-in-Publication Data
The Playwrights' Center monologues for men / edited by Kristen Gandrow and Polly K. Carl.
    p. m.
    ISBN 0-325-00742-X (alk. paper)
    1. Monologues.   2. Acting—Auditions.   3. Men—Drama.   4. American drama—20th century.   I. Gandrow, Kristen.   II. Carl, Polly K.
III. Playwrights' Center (Minneapolis, Minn.)
    PN2080.P62   2005
    812'.04508054—dc22   2004025906

Editor: Lisa A. Barnett
Production: Elizabeth Valway
Typesetter: Kim Arney Mulcahy
Cover design: Jenny Jensen Greenleaf
Manufacturing: Louise Richardson

Printed in the United States of America on acid-free paper
09 08 07 06 05 VP 1 2 3 4 5

*To Barbara Field, John Olive, Tom Dunn, Erik Brogger,
and Jon Jackoway, the founders of the Playwrights' Center.
What a great idea!*

Contents

Creating the Life of Theater

The Playwrights' Center in Minneapolis is celebrated by emerging and established playwrights as an essential artistic home. We nurture artistic excellence and new visions of theater, foster playwright initiative, and advocate for playwrights and their work. We continue to develop a community for new work in the American theater.

The genesis of new plays is with playwrights—and monologues like those represented here. This collection showcases the spectrum of writing for the theater that is crafted by Playwrights' Center members.

Within these pages you'll find an imaginary childhood friend grown to adulthood; the powerful effect of the rodeo on a man's life; a "Dolphin Boy" exploiting his disability; and an old salt explaining his feelings and defining a friendship. You'll enjoy resonance between the words of a jockey and a politician, an academic and a heckler, a circus performer, a drag queen, and a mascot. You'll engage with the dreams and struggles of travelers, farmers, fathers—the everyday life and death that confronts each of us.

Playwrights write for *live* theater, for actors in front of an audience. These monologues feature outstanding writing for actors to seize, speak from the heart, and bring the words' actions to life for us. These are the words playwrights create and need to hear "in the actors' mouths." The monologues in these pages are artistic tools for actors that allow hilarious, poignant, passionate, and spirited interpretation. When performed for acting classes and auditions, these monologues virtually guarantee unique material—a bonus for everyone involved.

New plays—and especially monologues like these—provide us with a powerful collective experience. In the theater with other people, strangers and artists alike, we share a space where new worlds are imagined and the complex issues of our lives are examined.

The aesthetically diverse voices of Playwrights' Center members speak with conviction, honesty, and humor. A collection of our playwrights' monologues for women is available in a companion volume. This set of books belongs on the shelves of every actor, theater educator, and playwright. We hope you'll agree!

—Kristen Gandrow

A Destination for Playwrights

The Playwrights' Center in Minneapolis has been developing new plays for the stage for nearly thirty-five years. During that time we have had the opportunity to work with some of the most important American playwrights, including August Wilson, Mac Wellman, Naomi Wallace, Lee Breuer, Craig Lucas, Theodora Skipitares, Suzan-Lori Parks, and Jeffrey Hatcher, to name a few. Plays by our writers have won every major award in the American theater.

Our presence as a vital new play development center is thriving, and our impact is reaching ever further to playwrights at every level of their careers. The center annually awards more than two hundred thousand dollars in fellowships and grants. We are a national membership organization with more than four hundred members across the United States—some writing their first plays and others winning their first Obie award. The center is a creative home where playwrights can explore writing for the theater, emerge as new dramatic voices beginning to be heard throughout the country, and sustain professional careers as dramatists. The vital and engaging environment at the center offers playwrights encouragement and the creative freedom to imagine theater in every shape and genre.

The center's programs provide many varied opportunities for playwrights. Every Wednesday night at our roundtable, Twin Cities professional actors volunteer to read a new play, and a playwright-filled audience offers feedback and answers questions from the evening's featured playwright. Additionally, our playwrights lab brings collaborators together throughout the year for workshops and readings. Each year, produced plays throughout the country have their start at the center—as a seed of an idea or exercise in a playwriting class, a cold reading of a first draft, a staged reading, or a workshop.

We recently awarded a Playwrights' Center McKnight Residency and Commission to Craig Lucas. His development process at the center encapsulates our strength in bringing new plays to the American stage. Craig started with a proposal, which led to a first draft. Joined by some very talented local actors and a director from New York who is familiar with Craig's work, we spent an intense dramaturgical month workshopping the play with all of the collaborators. Rehearsals began two months later, and we launched a modest production. One year later, *Small Tragedy* won the Obie award for best new American play after moving from the Playwrights' Center to an Off-Broadway stage. Craig said of his time at the center, "I've never had a better experience developing a new play anywhere, in any venue, in this country or elsewhere."

Our members are the heart of the organization. The stories of the center's impact on playwrights' lives are myriad. Melanie Marnich tells of living in Cincinnati, working in an advertising agency, and becoming a member of the Playwrights' Center before she ever wrote a play. She knew she would eventually make her way to the stage, and regular communication with an organization for playwrights provided exactly the inspiration she needed. Since becoming a member, she has won numerous fellowships through the center, including a Jerome in 1999 and 2000 and a McKnight Advancement Grant in 2001 and 2004. Melanie's plays have won multiple awards and have been produced around the country, including twice at the Humana Festival and Off-Broadway.

Lee Blessing has said, "Without the Playwrights' Center, I never would have been a playwright." Referring to the center's pluralism, Blessing said he considers the center "one of the most important opportunities in the entire field of the arts." Our openness to new voices and new forms creates a palpable energy that spreads across the nation and infiltrates theaters around the country. It's impossible to see new plays without encountering the center's impact on the field.

—Polly K. Carl

THE PLAYWRIGHTS'
CENTER
MONOLOGUES
FOR MEN

The Importance of Golf
from *The Fattest Man*
in the World Lives Upstairs

JANET ALLARD

JACK practices putting in the living room. He holds a golf club. He addresses his wife.

JACK: Irene, If you're looking for something to do, you could iron my shirt.

(Pause)

I've got a meeting tomorrow and no shirts.

(Pause)

You're not *reacting*, are you?

You're not reacting to what I just said about ironing my shirt because you're a woman and I was just—

Irene, if I were another woman, and we were living in here together and we were sisters or something and I asked you to iron my shirt you wouldn't *react* would you—you wouldn't be upset.

No you wouldn't. No, right, or if we weren't married, I mean, if I were just over here as your friend, and I asked you friend to friend, if you could help me out and iron my good shirt because I was too busy—playing golf, perfecting my stroke—and needed a little help. Because I was busy playing golf. But because you're my wife and a woman and I'm a man and I ask you—Oh Jesus! You don't think it's valid to be busy playing golf. You don't think that's a valid type of thing to be busy at. Well let me tell you something, Irene. Let me tell you something. It's very important that I get this ball in this hole. That I learn how to get this ball in this hole from this distance.

I

Because if I can do that I will be at a great advantage and right now I am at a distinct disadvantage because I cannot for the life of me get this ball into this hole at this distance and I'm losing a lot of money and that's not the half of it, I'm losing a great deal of money and respect and business and that's not even the half of it. I have to buy rounds of drinks for men who can get that ball in that hole from that distance and they have better suits, Irene, better suits and nicer shirts and because of that, I am at a distinct disadvantage. Because I want a cherry in my martini instead of an olive and everyone at the table laughs at that, and everyone thinks that's funny, but I like cherries, and that's not the half of it, I don't drink, I never drink, until now because that's business and knowing that an olive goes in that glass and a cherry goes in this one is important, and asking for a cherry in the olive glass is funny. And it's pitiful, so I ask for olives, and I hate green olives with the red squishy—and to float it in your drink—God! Do you understand Irene. All I want is a friend to help me iron my shirt while I'm here practicing my stroke. That's all I want is a friend but I will iron my own fucking shirt because you have some kind of reaction when I ask you to do it. Some kind of reaction.

Saving You from *Untold Crimes of Insomniacs*

JANET ALLARD

THE COP: I know you want me to ask you in, Annie, because you are standing on my front stoop with a suitcase, but I'm not going to ask you in this time, Annie.

You know I get important calls in the middle of the night, Annie, I get calls where someone's just been shot—real emergencies, where people are dying here. Are you dying here? When the phone rings alarms go off, I am up and ready for action. This better not be a false alarm Annie.

Annie, you know and I know, we both know that this is not about me. You're not here because you were dying to see me. You're here because you want me to save you. It's not about me Annie, it's about you. And I have more self-respect than that. I have finally arrived at the decision that I have to respect myself. You have to respect yourself, too, Annie, because no one else will.

I'm done, Annie. I need to start a new life.

I need someone who needs me 24-7. Not someone who wants me sometimes, needs me sometimes to put out a fire someone else started. I am not a fireman. I have a lot to give, but—I shot a kid today, Annie. Is he gonna live? Is he gonna die? I don't know, I'm calling the hospital every hour on the hour to find out. It was a mistake, Annie, but what good does that do him. What good does it do anyone to know it was a mistake. None. Sometimes people make mistakes. Irreparable mistakes.

I care, Annie, I care very much.

And I feel like a real bad guy here for not letting you in. When I see that you are in a bad spot and you need a place to go. And I hope you can forgive me. But I need to do what I need to. I have made a decision here, Annie. And that decision is final.

I am in love with you, Annie, and that is why I can't see you anymore.

Sometimes there is an empty space within you and it feels like a black hole. But you need to go through that, Annie, you need to experience that empty place in order to allow something new to come into it. You need to create a vacuum to be filled.

This isn't working out here, Annie.

You and I both know it.

We aren't right for each other.

Because for whatever reason,

I know you love me, Annie, but you don't quite love me enough.

I need to start anew Annie. And so do you.

Okay?

Okay?

Excerpt from
Voices Underwater

ABI BASCH

ALBERT: My dearest darling Wife of Another, society life must dull your senses daily, dream of me at night? I only hope. All the fetes, the "Welcome Home, Generals," the tending to abolitionists and senators, however do you find the time to dream at night of your poor little soldier in the fields braving the brave so you might feed your senators fat? Do you miss my misbehaving tongue? I only hope.

Close my eyes at night, imagine you safe and pristine in my dreams. Artillery fire shakes the ground on which I sleep. I shake.

(Albert rips the letter to shreds.)

You may tell your fat senators I fought the front of Grant's charge against Vicksburg. Marched the frontlines against Bedford Forest in Mississippi, then on through the Battle of Nashville, Battle of Mobile, watched as my company members, friends and brothers, fell around me, pierced through, bloodied, blown apart by gunshot, by cannons, by fire, sometimes by disease by rotting limbs. You may ask your fat senators where were their sons as I watched this my family, murdered in a field, gone now every last one. One by one, now spread in mass graves unmarked.

(Albert rips the letter to shreds.)

I am a veritable war hero, fought more than forty battles unscathed. Until three days ago. Now wounded, now taken in hospital, trapped in an attic space, overcrowded with the wounded and the dead, rains make the air heavy, the stench of rotting flesh weighs me down, I am dying.

(Albert rips the letter to shreds.)

Home Is What the Hat Is

ALAN M. BERKS

A man onstage twirls a hat up in the air and paces.

The man I worked for in Israel gave me this hat to keep the sun and rain out of my eyes while I herded his goats for him. I love this hat. It's a magic hat. I used to wear it all the time when I traveled.

(Puts the hat on his head)

When I flew back to the United States through Amsterdam, the customs agent at O'Hare pulled me aside and asked, "Hey, you smoke."

"Yes," I said. "Do you need a cigarette?"

"No," he said. "Not that kind of smoke."

"O," I said. "O, no, it makes me paranoid."

So he asks me what I did in Amsterdam. I said, uh, I, the weekend—I went to the Van Gogh Museum.

"Van Gogh Museum," he said. "The Van Gogh Museum?"

"The Van Gogh Museum," I said. "Have you been?"

"You're telling me you spent the weekend in Amsterdam—in Amsterdam—at the Van Gogh Museum."

"Yes. It's a very good museum."

He notices my shoes. "Where d'you get those shoes?" he asks.

"In Israel. I was hiking all the time and my other shoes—"

"You didn't declare them," he said.

"O, right. Right. I forgot about them 'cause they're on my feet like a part of my body—"

"Let me see them."

(Bends over to take off his shoes)

He tells me that he has the right to confiscate my shoes and cut them open to see if I'm smuggling drugs.

I tell him, "I'm sorry. I don't have any other shoes. I'd have to walk through Chicago naked."

Then he tells me that he can have me strip searched. For lying.

(Standing up and extending shoes toward audience and customs agent)

I told him I couldn't be more truthful if I was naked.

He tells me, "Your shoes—smell like goat shit."

I tell him he's right.

Then he asked me if I knew why he pulled me aside at the baggage claim.

I said no.

He said, "Because that hat looks so stupid, I figured you must have been stoned."

(Takes off hat and puts it in hand with shoes)

He smiles and, I swear I think he said, "Welcome home."

Reed's Site from
The Donner Gold

ANNE BERTRAM

Setting: The internet

REED NOLAND: I am descended from survivors.

They handed down stories—not the one most people want to hear.

They handed down stories of a wagon filled with gold.

September, 1846. Eighty-seven people, with twenty ox-drawn wagons, struggle across the great salt flats of Utah. The fine sand clutches every footstep, drags at every wheel.

James Frazier Reed has to make a decision. He looks at his three heavy wagons. He looks at his panting oxen, his anxious wife and children. He takes his hat off, wipes his forehead, and looks west.

Anything will grow in California. He knows this from Captain Hastings's little book. "Apples, pears, peaches, plums, cherries and grapes, oranges, lemons, citrons, dates, and pomegranates." He read this in December in Illinois.

He will do what he must to get where he is going. What is a writing desk, a box of medicines, what is the set of Sunday china, compared to California? What are three heavy bags of gold?

He takes the wheels from one of his wagons. He loads it with his goods. He covers it with boards and heaps the bitter sand upon it. He sketches the landmarks. He beckons to his family and leads the oxen onward. Onward to the mountains and a winter of starvation. They know what they want. Apples, peaches, plums; lemons, citrons, pomegranates. They will do what they must.

I have the stories. I have the sketch. I have fifteen years of research which suggests that that heap of sand may very well still lie there, undisturbed. You have an urge to keep visiting this page. You have a vision of the great salt flats. You have some money saved, enough for plane tickets, camping equipment, a four-wheel drive with a trailer.

You know what you want.

You can contact me. Click here.

Excerpt from *Definition*

JANEA RAE BOYLES

CARL, a macho, late thirties New Yorker debates whether he should choose his longtime lucky cologne over his new girlfriend.

CARL: I'm a person who does things a certain way to keep his universe in line. One thing happens and bam! It causes another thing to happen. You may not even see it going that way, but I guarantee you, it's for a reason and there is something behind it. The day my girl Penny first walked up and talked to me, I was rubbing a shiny penny I had found. She said to me, she said, "Nuts or pretzels, sir?" I nearly melted right there in first class all over her blue pumps. We go out on a date and have a great time. We go out on another date and have another great time. Things are going along pretty damn great. Until our third date! She tells me I can't wear my cologne anymore. I don't know what to say. I can't even think when she says this to me. Now ordinarily, I would say, "No way, Jose!" But, this girl, Penny, I mean she is special. I got such a feeling about her. I've been wearing this cologne since I was nineteen. The day I bought it was the same day I literally bumped into Raquel Welch on the street coming out of a revolving door. I was helping her pick up her things, and she says, "Oh, nice cologne." I swear it was her. So when Penny tells me I can't wear my lucky cologne anymore, my world is like turned upside down on my level. I wish I knew what was going on in her mind. She told me the smell of my cologne reminds her of something bad that happened to her a really long time ago. Something really bad. That's all she would say. Now what can a guy say to that? So, I'm gonna have to wait. I'm gonna wait until she's ready to tell me more. I gotta do it. I gotta do without the cologne and trust that whatever is going on with my lucky Penny has nothing to do with me and everything to do with her.

Excerpt from *Ritual*

RICHARD BROADHURST

ASMA, seventeen years old

ASMA: I had this stuffed monkey when I was little—Ali Baba. Took it everywhere. Couldn't sleep without it. Some time right after I turned five my mother woke me in the middle of the night. She pulled me out of bed so quickly I didn't have time to take Ali Baba with me. I was wrapped in a blanket and rushed out of the house. There was a lot of screaming. We ended up in a house across the street. I wasn't upset until I realized I had left Ali Baba behind. I begged my father to let me go back for my monkey. He slapped me hard across the face. It was the only time my father ever hit me. I was too shocked to cry and my father picked me up immediately and held me. I looked over and saw my mother and sister huddled in a corner. I asked where my older brother was and was told to be quiet. I looked out the window and saw this giant machine crash into the side of the house where my bedroom had been. I was surprised at how easily the wall caved in . . . like Play-Doh. The next day we returned to the dust that had been our home and began sifting through the remains. My mother would cry every time she found a piece of broken pottery or an old photograph. Finally I found this little brown button. It was Ali Baba's eye. I was so excited. I showed my mother. I thought it might make her feel better. She smiled, spit on her white scarf and wiped dirt from my cheek. I cleaned off the button and jammed it into my pocket. I held onto the button for years. Over time I forgot what it was and why I had it, but one day I reached into my pocket and it was gone. I probably left it in my pants and it got washed away in the laundry. I cried. And I remembered everything.

Freedom Stakes from
Pure Confidence

CARLYLE BROWN

SIMON: Caroline! Come on in girl. I'm riding this barrel in the freedom stakes. Freedom against Slavery, match race, winner takes all. Simon Cato on Freedom and the Bondage Man riding Slavery. And with a tap of the drum they're off. Oops, Freedom got a bad start, Slavery's in the lead. Coming around the first turn it's Slavery by a length. Freedom holding steady, storm clouds are a coming, and the patter of rain falling on the track. Down the backstretch the thunder begins to roll as the rain starts pouring down. It don't look good for Freedom, 'cause Slavery is a mudder. The dirtier and more mucky it gets the better she likes it and she's running like a hellhound on judgment day. Coming around the far turn it's Slavery by half a length, Freedom is gaining. Passing the grandstand it's Freedom and Slavery neck and neck, Slavery on the inside, Freedom on the outside, side by side, not a sign a daylight between 'em. "Give it up," says the Bondage Man, "You can't win today." "Ain't no way," says Simon Cato, "You soon to be looking at my horse's ass." And Slavery is running, and Freedom is running, and the mud is flying and you can't tell which rider is white and which rider is black or which horse is which. First it's Slavery by a nose, then Freedom by a nose, now it's Slavery by a neck and then Freedom by a neck, back and forth round the near turn and down the back stretch. The Bondage Man got his spurs dug into Slavery's sides, and he's whipping her flanks like the devil beating off justice. And Simon Cato is riding low and biding his time. And coming round again on the far turn he lays down his whip

13

and calls on Freedom to give him all her best and she starts to running like pure moonshine swallowing down your throat, smooth, then hot, then burning. Coming off the turn it's Freedom by a half a length, Freedom by a whole length, Freedom by two lengths, three lengths, four lengths. It's Freedom and Simon Cato the winners . . . Slavery to place and ain't nobody to show. And the crowd roars. *(Simon makes a sound of a crowd roaring.)* Mister Reporter Man from the *Louisville Gazette* asks Simon, "Boy how you win that race?" Go on Caroline, you be the reporter. Ask me how I won that race on Freedom.

Excerpt from *Little Vines*

CORY BUSSE

A hospital. A beleaguered-looking father-to-be wearing hospital scrubs picks himself up off the floor. MITCH *(thirties) rubs his head. He looks back to where he lay. He's embarrassed.*

MITCH: Jesus. I've never seen that much blood. I'm such a wuss. We're expecting. Hell, I guess we're not expecting anymore . . . now it's imminent. We're in the home stretch. Last week, we were expecting. Today, it's just a matter of a little while. I told her I was going to pass out. I mean, I didn't really tell her. Because then, when it happened, she'd say that it was a self-ful-filling prophecy. That I psyched myself out and made myself pass out. But I knew I was going to. I even tried to tell one of the nurses, but she was too concerned with Jenny to bother with what I was saying. Good for her. That's right. That's how it should have been.

(Looking back, chuckling)

Of course, I'll bet she wishes she would have paid a little more attention to me now. Look at me. I look like a pile of dirty laundry; a fat pile of dirty laundry. "Stay up by her head," they told me. "Just keep looking in her eyes; you'll be fine." That was the trouble, and I knew it was going to be.

(He looks upstage back toward where he fell. He turns and faces the audience again.)

I am so going to hear about this. I'll never live it down, you know. She comes from a long line of teasers, see. She's got four brothers. They're all really bright. Quick witted. Somebody'll get their hands on smelling salts as a gag gift for me next Christ-mas. And nickels to donuts says that when her dad carves the turkey or ham or Christmas goose, somebody will throw a glass of water in my face. "Don't pass out, Mitch!"

(He winces.)

I've always had a low tolerance for gore. Hollywood violence doesn't phase me. I can watch vampires cut off the heads of zombies all day long. But drive me over a bit of fresh road kill, and I get an attack of the willies so bad it feels like my spine is part of a kick line. Channel surfing, land on the Surgery Network, and I'm a puddle. Real people, you know? Real pain. I can't do that. One time, I was walking down a sidewalk in Washington, D.C. It was this beautiful spring day. The annual Kite Festival was going on down on the Mall. Naturally, we were all looking up. I caught sight of this girl. She was really pretty. Pretty enough that I was looking at her and not at the kites. Anyway, this woman was walking toward us, staring up at these amazingly complicated kites diving and soaring above the Smithsonian when she tripped and fell. Which would have been bad enough, but it happened so suddenly that she didn't get her hands out in front of her to break her fall. She just went splat. Face down. Right into the concrete. I ran over to her. She lay still for a second, then she propped her forehead on her arms. I asked her if she was okay. Jenny was already digging in her purse for the cell phone so we could call the Park Police and get an EMT there. When the woman straightened up, her nose gushed blood. Just this impossible amount of red erupted from her face. I took one step toward a woman pushing a stroller to ask if she had a towel or a diaper or something we could use to stop the bleeding . . . when I swooned.

(Laughing)

I think swooned is exactly the right way to put it. A knight in shining armor. So, yeah, I've got a really low tolerance for physical pain. In others, anyway.

(Points to where he picked himself up from the floor a moment ago)

See? That's me . . . and I think I'm going to need stitches over that left eye. Yeah. Emotional pain I can cope with. If someone is sad, even if they're completely lost, I'm okay. I get stronger. My inclination is to help. No matter how bad things may be, I feel like I can offer comfort. Reassurance. At least sympathy. Like today. A friend of mine was killed in a car accident. Talk about physical pain. It doesn't escape me that this guy and I were the same age . . . he was a contemporary. We cruise around in our twenties and thirties, and we get so wrapped up in our lives and where they're going that we forget that we all have a common, ultimate destination. This little person that I've helped to bring into this world is now on that same path. And while I try not to live my life worrying about my own mortality, I do. I don't mean to sound morbid, but I have to say, knowing that this fit, able guy who wasn't any more than a couple of months older than I am, is now just an empty, broken vessel. It scares the hell out of me. I hadn't known about this guy's death for ten minutes when Jenny's water broke. And I'll let you in on another little secret. Just being here makes me want to cry. Here we are, twelve hundred miles from anyone we know. We've made friends, but it's hard to get close to new people in a new city. When we checked her in, the nurse started asking me questions. They wheeled her away and started getting her ready. They sat me down and just started grilling me. They were very nice about it. But it was, What's her date of birth? Who's her insurance provider? What's her social security number? Like she's going to have to pay taxes while she's in here or something. I felt my head start to swim. Then it hit me. If anything goes wrong—if anything happens—they're not going to call her mother. They're going to call me. I'm the "who to call in case of emergency." I'm the one who gets to worry about her. It's the first time that that's ever occurred to me. It got me. And I think Jenny saw it. I think she knew.

(Pause)

Watching others in physical pain. That's different. I come apart. It runs through me. It finds my spine and shoots this flood of—it feels like what I can only characterize as liquid dread—into me. My stomach knots. I feel my sphincter ache. Don't laugh. I do. And it's not a pleasant experience. I hate seeing others in physical pain because physical pain always brings

17

with it fear. Desperation. Outright panic. I never had a chance. "Just keep looking in her eyes," they told me. Right. That's just the place to look for it. Pain. Panic. Fear. And what's worst, what gets me every time, is that I know that the fear is mine.

(Looks back again)

They're reviving me now. I've got to go. *(Pause)* Fuck, the first photos are going to be of me with our newborn and a bandage on my skull. And now I get to worry about both of them. Save my seat. I'll probably be back here soon.

Excerpt from
We Are Not These Hands

SHEILA CALLAGHAN

LEATHER is clean-looking and weary. He clutches a leather bag and speaks into a hand-held tape recorder.

LEATHER: It isn't it isn't it isn't. Okay. Just, and the noise, the the bling bling bling bling bling bling bling bling bling bling and me sitting there as though work were actually something that could, that that could be DONE. That I could DO. But. And and the PEOPLE, and the PORN, porn everywhere. So highly illegal. But then I, then so is the café I'm I imagine. But. So, so some guy next to me, not one single tooth in his head, begging me for coins, so he can keep, um keep on, and and this girl, this, couldn't have been older than, what, with this get-up from I-don't-know and drinking Coke from a can and looking around with these wild eyes, these wild eyes and and I'm trying to WORK. You know? And it's not like I have, there's somewhere else, not that I okay, no. No need to be negative. I'm not here for negative. And um. But with the dirt and the stench and people with the rotting teeth and the, sometimes like a smell like curdled milk, so, so yeah so negativity is just another, to add to the. So. And it's the only café with internet access in twenty-five miles, so. You know three people threw up on the bus to the café tonight. Bad shocks, or. Or maybe the appalling diets of the, which would explain the the teeth, but. So they just leaned over and spewed right there, right in the aisle. Okay one woman opened her window but the other two. Forty-minute bus ride, Mother. And this happened relatively shortly after the after we left. And of course it was freezing, no no heat on of course on the bus, uh and of course the all the windows, the glass was cracked, and. People SMOKING ON THE BUS. I mean I just. And people spit here, they spit everywhere, hawk and spit. On floors. I mean floors of BUILDINGS, Mother. Hhuh. And my hostel? Shutters on the windows that don't even LATCH. And no mirrors, like ANYWHERE. And and of course no heat, and I asked the boy for extra blankets and he he just.

(Banging from outside. LEATHER covers the microphone of the recorder.)

ONE. SECOND. PLEASE.

(Banging stops. Back to the recorder.)

Sorry, I'm in the, I'm in one of those, one of those. Things. Anyway. Yeah. So. Ahhh. Forget it. Oh the bathrooms, or I don't suppose you can even CALL them, that, there's no bath, a just a hose with a drain in the ground, and hot water? I have to shower at noon because at least then the sun MIGHT be hitting the ground at the perfect angle so that the pipes can get warm so that the, the water can heat up, and toilets? No. A TROUGH, Mother. With these little cinderblock walls that come up to your knees and a trough that you STRADDLE, okay, you squat over, over the trough in a straddle and let it, let whatever, dangle from you until you, and, and NO toilet paper, and of course if someone is squatting in the stall next to you they can just watch your stuff float by beneath them, and you PRAY that the bucket next to you is filled with enough water to wash it away. Because if it isn't. Well. I mean I mean. How much could plumbing actually cost? What is this whole, okay preserving antiquity is swell and all but DO PEOPLE REALLY NEED TO SEE MY POOP?

(Banging again from outside)

You know. Working here isn't. Easy. Eating here isn't easy. Nothing. Not that I thought it would be, but. Again. No negativity. Because, because the sun is shining and the, I haven't been robbed and I'm I don't have dysentery, so. I think. I think I'm gonna cry.

(He shuts off the tape and begins to cry.)

Hold This

SHEILA CALLAGHAN

Hold this. Here. Take it. Hold it. Take it. Hold it.

No, he says.

Take it. Put it with the other ones.

No, he says. They aren't alive, he says.

Don't think about that. They're sleeping.

They are not sleeping, he says. Their chests flutter when they sleep.

Listen. I can't pay someone to do it. Do it. Take it. Hold it.

So he holds it. In his right hand. Cream-yellow puff of fuzz. Orange pencil-point beak. Its chest does not flutter.

Voices are banging behind him. Commercial people making their commercial. His mother's voice the loudest among them. "We only have nine more. Try not to give them *all* heart attacks."

But most of them do not die from heart attacks. Only two. Most of them die from the heat of the commercial lamps. Baby chicks can thrive in sunlight, in moonlight, in infrared light that does not exceed temperatures of seventy degrees. They cannot survive eight hundred watts of stage lighting.

So he holds it. In his right hand. He thinks of. An infrared light bulb. The black X's he drew on all the eggs that were about to hatch. The pickle jar lid filled with marbles and drinking water, marbles to keep the chicks from drowning. The new velour sofa his mother ordered after she was told how much the agency would be paying her.

He hears a man's laugh behind him, a pointy, pick-axe laugh. "It got cooked. This must be how they make chicken nuggets."

His mother does not laugh. She contemplates her son over the frames of her Ray-Bans. This is the first time it occurs to her that he might be gay.

He lays the dead chick into a cardboard box lined with newspaper. He makes sure its head is aligned with the heads of all the other dead chicks, so they might dream of one another. He lifts the box and walks towards the house. Something twitches inside. Still alive! Startled, he trips on a lighting cable. Newspaper lifts, twelve yellow puffs soar through the air in fuzzy arcs. Hit the concrete almost noiselessly. But not. Pat. Pat pat-pat. Pat. They bounce lightly.

Twelve yellow puffs on the concrete. None of them twitching.

He steps away from the dead chicks. He walks over to the water spigot. Retrieves a metal bucket. Fills it with water and bleach. Thrusts his right hand into it. Scrubs the hand with an iron brush.

His mother shouts his name.

He scrubs. Metal in his throat, the taste of fear. He scrubs.

His mother shouts.

He scrubs.

He scrubs.

Excerpt from *Findings Uncertain: A Play about Adoption in Three Pieces*

BETH CLEARY

TIM (thirties to forties) is riding on a train from his father's funeral. He is drawn into conversation with two strangers, who discuss immigration and dreams of origins.

TIM: Him. Roasted sweet potatoes with red onion and corn. Ha, leftovers. He cooked, learned to cook when he retired. It came in handy after Mom died. He started to travel, on his railroad pension, to learn about food. He said he was going back to school, the railroad almost got all of him but not his stomach, and he was going to let that gut of his lead the way, into the school of living he'd say. It did. He died with a refrigerator full of food that he made, labeled, and dated. After the funeral my aunt started to throw it out. I saw her and grabbed her arm. "No!" She said it would spoil. And wasn't it a bit morbid of me? I grabbed stuff out of her hand and took as much of it as I could. I shipped all the canned stuff to myself. In the hotel room I ate from the containers . . . of Dad . . . he had made that food . . . and I cried and I vomited. I ate and I cried and I vomited. (*Pause*) This. These containers are what I have left. Pacing myself. Like a horse pacing out the perimeter of his fence. When this is gone, I'm an orphan.

Excerpt from *Heckler*

BILL CORBETT

This one-actor play is in the form of a spoken diary, all monologue.

June 10

Strange doings today. Benjamin picked me up. He was excited about his first day as my "apprentice." I reminded him that I wasn't teaching him to be a silversmith or to tan hides or anything—that this was very metaphysical work. We went to the pro-family rally downtown, rescheduled from last week.

The people running the rally were using the word "family" like a blunt instrument. Especially the main speaker, a tall, lean, but somehow jowly man, whom I'll call Mr. Angry. Mr. Angry's words about "the family" were all sweet and gooey; but he was a joyless sort, and seemed like the type who'd make his kids march around the yard all day wearing nothing but burlap.

Anyway, I was about to engage Mr. Angry on several points, but as I was doing my usual minute of deep breathing—to prep the diaphragm—someone else started razzing the man.

A *rival*!

And this fellow was good—a bit older than me, and quite handsome, really. His casual-neat wardrobe seemed perfect for the task at hand, making me question for the first time my own strategy of *the suit*. (Sidebar: overstatement?) Anyway, many in the crowd were really rooting for him as he took on Mr. Angry.

And there was even someone *filming* him! A man with a sizable movie camera. He focused ever closer on Mr. Casual-Neat; he had found a star!

This really made me jealous, I am ashamed to say. But I must admit, Mr. Casual-Neat was really hitting the mark, questioning Mr. Angry's points with intelligence, vigor, and a charismatic warmth. Mr. Angry was briefly on the ropes. Mr. Casual-Neat disputed his use of statistics, questioning his claim that the majority of young men who grow up fatherless wind up as chronic masturbators. Mr. Angry had nothing to cite about his masturbation facts except, quote, "My experience with young people at our church," which was an unfortunate way of putting it, given the subject. Segueing nicely on the mention of church, Mr. Casual-Neat went on to question Mr. Angry's interpretation of the Book of Leviticus.

And here Mr. Casual-Neat dropped a bombshell: he was a *minister*! A pastor of a church! A man of the Lord, a kind, thoughtful, respectable man, and a good-looking one at that, out there on my beat. It made me feel proud, but also more than a little threatened. I thought, "What if he's better than me?"

Alas, dear diary, he simply wasn't.

His argument over Leviticus was a tactical error. Mr. Angry was quite prepared on this point: very knowledgeable about the Old Testament, especially the judgment and punishment-related parts. His face softened a bit, and he made a flawed, but seemingly well-reasoned argument about Leviticus' condemnation of masturbation, even allowing—and this surprised me—even allowing for the fact that some of the Bible might be open to interpretation. The Reverend Casual-Neat was disappointing in his response: tepid, logically circular, and not nearly as versed in the Bible. He must be a Unitarian, I thought. He even misquoted one of Paul's letters to the Colossians—misquoted badly, and it was quickly corrected by Angry, who had a whole mess of Good Books on hand to prove it. The reverend had lost face. People were turning away from him, as was the camera, ready to refocus exclusively on Angry. He had lost the All-Seeing Eye.

And here's where I jumped into the breach, my friends. While I confess to a shameful *schadenfreude* at seeing my rival the Rev go down, I couldn't let the repellent Mr. Angry win the day. But how? Casual-Neat's strategy had failed. And I knew less about the Bible than I should have. I cursed my lack of preparedness, and contemplated going home to do some studying.

But then I took a nice luxurious breath, and gave over to the Universe. As usual, inspiration came from Nowhere—or rather, from the collective net of consciousness that connects us all, a kind of Everywhere, but which I prefer to call "Nowhere," as it's more economical.

Without a nanosecond of thought, I started . . . *singing!* Singing a nonsense tune on loan from Nowhere, a vaguely ska-like ditty whose lyrics only occasionally touched down to earth as we know it:

> *"Big chicken lickin' angry purple plumber man*
> *He put all the marbles in de neighbor's garbage can . . ."*

My obscurantism managed to have the effect which nonsense often does: it made me seem more profound.

> *"All de chicken lickin' soldiers, they be plumbin' on de beat,*
> *Come to spill their may-o-naisse all over on de street!"*

Then, to my surprise, I started . . . *dancing!* Despite the fact that I had mainly held my body stiff as a board for my entire life, even as a baby, well—I was truly shaking my groove thang.

> *"Wants de ketchup and de mustard join his may-o-naisse-y world,*
> *Spread his purple plumbing ways to chicken lickin' boys and girls!"*

Somehow this was the right mix: an apparent insult to Mr. Angry, and yet the purest baloney, really.

Mr. Angry grew apoplectic, and before long started yelling at me: "Shut your heathen mouth!" This just loosened me up— I sang louder, and wiggled my keister with abandon, in a way that I daresay approached—well, *sexiness.*

It was not lost on me that the camera was now pointed my way.

Mr. Angry got more bent out of shape with every gyration I did. I matched his rage with silliness, and it teased out his real self. His eyes showed too much white, which never looks good; his lips disappeared entirely. He was metamorphosing into a Warner Brothers cartoon before our very eyes: I fully expected hot blasts of steam to start shooting out of his ears. He could simply not accept the fact that this dancing idiot in front of him had pulled focus and made it impossible for him to recapture it. A few fellow idiots stepped up and joined the dance. One guy called me "Snake Hips," a moniker I never thought I'd hear applied to myself.

> *"May-o-naisse in de chicken lickin' plumber man's pants,*
> *He just swallow a big boulder, so there no way he can dance!"*

Mr. Angry decided to take his ball and go home.

The crowd applauded. Applauded *me*.

The only sour note was one man who asked me what the hell I had against plumbers; that he was a plumber and damned proud of it. I apologized and said it wasn't meant literally and he said what the hell is *that* supposed to mean? I excused myself politely, and without even finding Benjamin, high-tailed it out of there.

I shouldn't be hanging around accepting plaudits anyway; that's unseemly.

June 11

A reflection on yesterday.

I confess I did leave the scene feeling quite heroic. But later I got depressed when I analyzed the day. Why was the crowd so . . . malleable? First they seemed captured by Mr. Angry, then by the Rev, then by Angry again, then by me. Like a crowd at a roller derby.

It's alarming that allegiances shift so rapidly, depending on who, ostensibly, is "winning." This was my very goal—to *win* these encounters—and yet I can't help feeling that my theories of Direct Transfer and Geometric Progression might be faulty.

Perhaps I should record them here, for posterity's sake:

My theory of Direct Transfer is based on the power of ancient gurus, who could actually transmit their consciousness to their followers, gently and lovingly. If I can apply that notion, if I am able to generate enough spirit in a live crowd, and charge enough of the atmosphere around me when speaking back to poisonous words, then I can affect others; *in*fect them, actually—in a good way, of course. This leads then to my related theory, of Geometric Progression: from here, others will Transfer Directly in the same fashion. So I can start an epidemic, perhaps even a pandemic, of optimism and full-throated courage, from the diaphragm, let loose out into the world!

Because people have lost their voices.

And I don't just mean metaphorically, I mean *physically*: Our vocal cords have atrophied from lack of use! One hundred years ago people used to sing around the piano together at night—just belting it out from the breadbasket, on-key or off didn't matter: they just . . . sang! Now we talk in low croaks, whispering apologetically. In some rare moments of justifiable outrage, when we can no longer physically contain the vibrations within, these moments when we briefly allow ourselves to open our mouths and let it rip, well, our own voices startle us! We immediately get scared by our own natural authority, and the responsibility which that implies, and our voices quickly start devolving back into a shaky petulance, often accompanied by a quick flip of the middle finger. This experience makes us eager to retreat further, back into anonymity, thinking, "Can't someone on television say this for me?"

Games

JEANNINE COULOMBE

Kept from contact with his now three-year-old son, TONY (mid-thirties) confronts his ex-wife, trying to convince her to allow some thread to exist between himself and his son.

No, wait. Please. Don't close the door. Please. Is he there? Wait. I'm not leaving. You can shut me out of *your* life, but you can't shut me out of *his*. He's my son. No matter how much you wish he wasn't, he is. You can't change that. No matter how much you try. He's half me as much as he's half you. Marrying this guy doesn't give Jake a father because he already has one. I'm right here. Wait. Please. I'm his father. I should have some right to say what I need to say. It doesn't matter what happened between us. Be mad at me. Be mad, I don't care. But please don't let his life go by without me in it. He doesn't even know me. Goddamn it. No, wait. I never wanted this to happen. Don't let this happen. Please. Look at me. I'm shaking just knowing he's behind that door. I'm so close to him and yet I . . . goddamn it. He doesn't even know who I am. And I should know him. He's my son. So . . . look . . . maybe you can't let me in right now. Okay. I don't have to meet him right now. Maybe we're not ready for that. But . . . but, I don't want him going to bed every night, thinking his father doesn't care. Even if he has some other guy there. He should at least know my voice. Can we start with that? Please. I bought this book. See? And uhmm . . . it was one I had when I was a kid and . . . I made this CD with me reading it, okay? So he can hear my voice. Wait. That's all I'm asking. No. Just take it. Please. No. Wait. Wait.

Fingerprinting a Corpse

STEPHEN J. CRIBARI

A minimalist stage. There is a table on which lays a corpse. Enter
SPEAKER, *wearing clinical white coat. Speaker takes position at stool*
behind table.

This corpse requires fingerprinting. You
Have to do it. There is no one else
On duty, and you have had the training. You
Will take a piece of what was someone else—
This finger—
    (Speaker holds up hand of corpse, then lets it drop.)

And give "Someone Else" a name.

Here is how you do it. Let me explain.
    (Speaker arranges scalpel, tube of lotion, ink pad, paper, jar of
formaldehyde.)

What you have to do is cut the skin
Off the finger. It's not hard to do.
When the body's dead the skin like parchment dries
And pulls away, recoiling from the bone.
    (Speaker holds up hand and makes two small, quick nicks
with scalpel at base of finger, slides off the tube of skin, then lets the
hand drop.)

Snip, snip, and it sloughs off just like that.
    (Continuing with monologue, Speaker displays skin, examines
it, then begins to soften it with lotion.)

It sounds distressing, but that's the easy part.

Softening this tube of dried-up skin,
Chiseled with the lines and hieroglyphs,
The I dids, I didn'ts, the maybes and what ifs
That make up someone's life, is a more delicate
Operation and not for the faint of heart.
One must act so carefully as one tries
To resurrect a finger once it dies.
To soften—
    (Tones of a cell phone are heard in the audience.)

I'm sorry, is that someone's cell phone?
    (Speaker peers among the audience, searching.)

If it's really necessary that you speak
While I'm talking—
    (Speaker identifies source of the disturbance.)

Excuse me, is it Ms. or Miss?
Please turn it off. Or leave. It's up to you.
Now, as I was saying, the skin like parchment dries
But with some care
    (Speaker appears intent and rubs lotion into the skin, with care.)

You make it viable
And this dead finger can yield reliable
Evidence of whom this person is,
Of whom he was—
    (Speaker looks at audience.)

Is it who or whom?
I never get it right. The verb "to be"
    (Speaker points with the finger-skin for emphasis.)

Cannot take an object, but is this who
Or whom the object of preposition or verb?

It's a small point, but with power to disturb
People who love detail, people who
Are meticulous, people who need to be
Accurate about a who or whom.
But I digress. To print reliable
Evidence of who this person was
(Yes, it's "who") you have to put him on.
You take this piece of "Someone Else's" skin
As if it were your own. Just slip it on,
Like this *(demonstrating)*, just slip it on and it will speak
Not in English Spanish French Italian or Greek
But in loops and whorls, in those lines and hieroglyphs
Unique to each person's I dids, I didn'ts and ifs.

In sum, to fingerprint a "Someone Else"
You have to remove his skin and put it on
And wear his skin as if it were your own.
   *(Speaker looks at finger with the skin on it, speaks to it slowly
and with great compassion.)*

This slip of skin, you can feel it down to the bone.
   *(Speaker resumes lecture tone and readies ink pad and finger-
print paper.)*

So remove the skin and soften, put it on,
Then *(demonstrating)* roll your finger in the indelible ink
And print your evidence of who you think
This "Someone Else," this person, is, or was.
   *(Speaker displays fingerprint, removes skin from finger and
puts it in a jar of formaldehyde.)*

This is all the easy, if somewhat indelicate, part.
   *(Speaker now addresses audience intimately, leaning on the
corpse as one might lean on a lectern.)*

But here: just let me ask you this. What if
One were to have put one's finger
Into one's own skin and felt it down to the bone?
Felt it, with a cold, detached dispassion
And understood one's self from the inside out
Utterly, clearly, beyond—without—a doubt?
Could you take your life with such compassion
As would let you soften it and try
It on for size, as if it were someone else?
And having identified your bit of self
Would you roll it in the indelible ink
And give us reliable evidence of who you think
He is, this "Someone Else," this you?
Could you tell us your dids, your didn'ts, your ifs?
You have to do it. There is no one else
On duty, and you have had the training. You.

(Speaker removes clinical white coat, takes stool, and sits downstage of corpse. Spot on speaker who faces audience.)

Here is how you do it.

(Speaker looks at audience with the look of someone about to confess a lifetime.)

Let me explain . . .

Excerpt from *The 13 Hallucinations of Julio Rivera*

STEPHEN R. CULP

FELONY JOYRIDE: Fashion. Fashion is the shield that protects us from the banal. Fashion is the caption in the scrapbook of decades. A buffer between the fabulousness we want to project, and the imperfect reality of our nakedness. Fashion is a transient hooker who shoots up in the closets of the rich and famous, and overdoses on the front doorsteps of the taste-impaired. Fashion is an off-the-rack limousine headed straight for tomorrow's paparazzi page. Fashion is the drag of saints and the straightjacket of the shallow. Above all, fashion is. And there isn't one fucking thing you can do about it. My name is Felony Joyride. I was brought up in Pensacola. Astroturf on the patio, acid-wash in the closet, and weenies on the grill. All that lack of taste can make a girl cranky. So one day I got me a wig, found me a Sasquatch-sized pair of pumps, and donned my ass in gay apparel. Glitter tube-top and silver lamé pedal-pushers. I walked into the living room and I started dancing a vogue on the coffee table. Daddy keeled over dead from a stroke on the spot, and I think Momma's still sitting in that Barcalounger with her jaw on her lap. Undaunted, I took me a strut down the main drag of ol' Pensacola. Made it about two blocks before that nice policeman stopped to talk about the weather. While he was pistol whipping me, I remembered that I wanted to get the fuck out of Pensacola. Sold my collection of movie star memorabilia, turned a couple of tricks, bought me a Pinto and never looked back. Got my name from the second and third billboards I saw as I made my escape. I skipped the first one . . . I had no intention of being known as Chevron Gaseteria. Politics work my nerves. Look, we all been through the mill. It's time to be fabulous and enjoy life. We only get one trip down that runway, girls. You better work.

Excerpt from *The 13 Hallucinations of Julio Rivera*

STEPHEN R. CULP

DANNY: Um, I thought about what you said about cutting a deal. So the shot is this . . . I'm gonna cooperate, okay? Tell you everything, all right? So, okay . . . here's the story. First of all . . . Doc Martens are nothin'. Just boots. We like 'em. That's all. They're just boots. And the hair. We like it short. That don't make us fuckin' nazis. Free country. We like our hair short. End of story. So anyway . . . I fell in with 'em last semester. I saw them around, and we started hangin'. We had the same ideas, us guys . . . same fuckin' boots. We were the Doc Marten Stompers. And you know, I fell in with 'em. We were a team. We didn't give a shit. We were fuckin' family. *(Pause)* Ev'ryone knows Vaseline Alley. Homos hang there. I seen it. Get this now. I don't hate homos, but do they hafta give each other head under the monkey bars? On the swing set? You know, where kids play. So that night we were kickin' around, chuggin' some Colt 45s, raisin' hell. And Double O starts in on how we gotta initiate the Stompers. Get a little wild, ya know? He's on this kick about how we gotta make a name for ourselves. Says we're gonna go stretch out a faggot or some homeless fuck. I thought we was just gonna rough 'em up a bit, ya know? So Double O grabs a hammer. I pick up this big-ass wrench. Eric gots a bottle of 45. And we hit the road. So we come to PS 69 and me and Eric and Double O cut into the schoolyard, through Vaseline Alley. And I'm getting this sick feeling in my gut, ya know? Eric has a plan.

36

We head across the b-ball court to a corner of the schoolyard, off in the shadows . . . a dead end. And me and Double O hide behind a Dumpster. Eric, the decoy . . . he disappears. And I start to feelin' real bad, like I don't wanna be there. But I look at Double O and he gives me the high sign, like everything's cool, ya know? And after what seems like fuckin' forever, Eric's back. And he got some guy following him. Part of me wants to scream at him . . . get the fuck outa here . . . but it's like I'm frozen. And what I see is Eric, all smiles and laughing and shit . . . and the guy follows him to the far corner. And Eric unzips his fly. And the guy goes to his knees. That's when me and Double O jump out, blocking his escape. He stands up . . . turns to face us. Pow! Eric blasts him back of the head with his bottle of 45. And Double O runs at him . . . swinging the claw-end of the hammer at the dude's head . . . real fast, like bam-bam-bam! And the guy . . . he's putting up a helluva fight. So that's when I run at him with the wrench . . . swing it like a baseball bat . . . catch the guy right smack in the face. I can't believe I done that, ya know? And meanwhile Double O's swingin' the hammer at his head like some crazy motherfucker. And everyone's screaming and I don't remember nuthin'. And poof! There's a knife in my hand. Swear to God I didn't know where the fuck that knife came from. Next thing I know is I see myself . . . like a movie. I'm sticking the knife in his back. It slip right in. But hard to pull back out. And the guy just sit down on the pavement. Hard. And he gots this surprised look on his face. And he so fucked up, but don't know it yet. His face is bleeding. His shirt's turning red. And next thing is I'm running faster and faster fastest I ever ran I see my shadow growing taller and taller running away from the light of the street lamp and I'm so fuckin' scared and I'm trying to catch my shadow and I'm scared shitless and I'll make you a bargain see I didn't want to fuck no one up I didn't know what was happening or what the fuck I was doin' . . .

(Despite his best efforts, Danny's macho facade dissolves. He starts to cry.)

Oh, god . . . I keep seeing his face, man. Keep seeing his fuckin' face. Can't believe it was me that night I can't believe it was my hand on that fuckin' knife and I had no fuckin' idea it would get so outa hand and what the fuck's gonna happen to me man? I wish I wasn't there, man . . . wish it wasn't me . . . keep seeing his fuckin' face, man . . . I keep seein' his fuckin' face . . .

Excerpt from *Perpetua*

VINCENT DELANEY

A campfire on the beach. Evening. EUGENE, an amateur sailor, late forties to mid-sixties and Audrey, whose father has died suddenly. Eugene shares a secret that transforms her sense of who he was.

EUGENE: About 2 P.M. we hit a southeaster, twenty knots, and the chop started. Ten foot swells, nothing we couldn't handle. We had all four sails out, making a good thirty knots, and Arthur was loathe to give in to weather. So we retracted the jib and shuttered the windows. Fog rolled in. Six P.M., Arthur came up and I went down to sleep. But I couldn't. We were rolling, side to side, I could hear all that water hissing at me. I was sure we were leaking. I guess I did sleep, because when I opened my eyes it was dark, and my legs were up above my head. Swells were thirty feet. The stern would lift, you'd hear it groan, and your face would press down into the bunk, toward the bottom. And we'd slam back into the trough, the hull shuddered, and you didn't know. Just didn't know. I made it up the stairs and I'm afraid I threw up. He thought that was funny. Do we really need more liquid, Eugene?

Swells from all sides. A wall of granite like I'd never seen before. Winds seventy knots, ice cold. I wanted to relieve him, the rudder must have been crushing on his hands, but he wouldn't hear of it. Told me to fix us supper. As if I could go back down there. I kept peeking to see if he was scared. Two minutes later the boat lifts, spins, and gets hit. Four windows shattered. We heard it, we knew what it was. I was watching his eyes. Nothing. Bilge pumps kicked in. I'm afraid I became upset. I may have cursed Arthur.

We couldn't get the sails down, the deck was swamped. The mast was croaking, ready to snap. The list was twenty degrees, we were hanging on a ledge, looking down at the froth. Arthur told me he was going to bail. Now bailing in a storm on a forty-foot boat is a curious idea. But he went down there.

Five A.M. Pitch black. Roaring in my ears. Eighty-five knots. Something ripped. Dinghy and radar, torn free. We put out a Mayday. Four hundred miles from anywhere. But we put it out. Then Arthur went to take a nap. I think he really did. I didn't want him so calm. I wanted him to scream, it's over. Pray to your maker. Embrace your watery grave. He took a nap.

I was alone, I was awake, or maybe not, and as we rose on the swell, I looked down and saw something. In our way. A whale, a house, I don't know, but it was in our way, and I needed to turn the boat. I jerked the rudder, and rolled us. I saw myself do it. Masts went into the sea. The crack was like my own soul crying out. The ship heeled over and lay on her side. She was gone.

Arthur came up, I don't know how, but he was there. He went over the side to rescue the life raft. I could have helped. I could have tried. I was frozen, holding the rigging, watching the water rise. And he came back for me. The deck went under, and he grabbed me, so hard I couldn't breathe, and swam me to the raft. The entire time I was kicking out, trying to drown him. And I knew it. I knew I was trying to kill him with me. And I couldn't explain it.

There was a time that I don't remember. We were blown loose, in the water. Chills. Then you get warm. It spreads, that warmth. I let go. Drifted down, where it was quiet. Calm. Arthur brought me back. Just his eyes, shining. I think, sometimes I think I died. And he made me come back.

Four days. Sun comes up, goes down. He sang, he talked, he joked. Said he was glad I'd sunk her. Time for a new boat. Next one would be bigger. And he wanted me to crew for him. When he said that I attacked him, I can't explain it, but I tried to choke him. Arthur was a lot bigger than me. He pinned me down, he didn't hurt me, he just chuckled.

On the fifth day I couldn't feel my body. The sky was bright, cold. Arthur wasn't moving. I crawled over to see. To his face. Pale. Scabs, sores, eyes puffy. Skin was red, infected. I touched him. Cold. His eyes opened. No words.

I knew then that I had killed him. He was going to die first, then I would, knowing what I'd done.

When they found us, when they pulled us out of that raft, half dead, I knew two things. That he forgave me. And that I knew this man. I knew who this man was.

(Silence. Eugene drinks.)

Trustworthy from
Training My Hands for War

MATT DI CINTIO

*LUKE, young-looking, sits in his room in a boarding house, smoking
a joint. He looks straight into a mirror.*

LUKE: I think I feel a midlife crisis coming on. And this is
highly unfortunate—*highly*—because I don't feel midlife coming on. Although who's to say? Perhaps I passed midlife many
years ago without even knowing it. Wouldn't that be awful,
terrible! . . . I'm telling *you* about my potential midlife and its
subsequently potential crisis because I feel we may have known
each other in the past. You do look terribly familiar, or should I
say terrifically familiar? I don't know. —I'm not so sure about
the red eyes, I'm not so sure about the dry eyes, the blindness of
them, they're new to this new scheme of things, but then again,
who's to say? . . . Don't misjudge me, please, it isn't often I talk
to just anybody I see in my bedroom who happens to look famil-
iarly a little like me; it simply isn't a frequent circumstance. —It
isn't a frequent circumstance that I talk to anybody in my bedroom. —I talk to you because I feel I can trust you—with conversation, with banter, witty or otherwise, but also with matters
of utmost urgency. Matters of inscrutable distress. Does it matter? I'm always doing impressions that nobody would recognize.
"So I said to my father, after twenty-nine years, twenty-nine I
said, so I said to him, You'd better get someone else in that
kitchen if she's gonna put shoes on!" Does that sound familiar,
do you get it? . . . Do you get this often? That people can trust
you? Do people—strangers—like me, I mean, do they approach
you and say, "My, aren't you the trustworthy type!" Because of
your face? Your face is so soft. It looks soft, it looks like it may

have been soft, at one point. Do you remember that point, times like this, when you look like this? I don't get it a lot, much, at all, that I'm trusted, that I look like I could be trusted. That my face is soft. But I suppose some people do . . . You don't? Come now, tell the truth . . . No? You swear that's the truth? People don't trust you? Swear it . . . They don't? . . . My, aren't you the trustworthy type . . . See. Now you got it from me. You've heard it from me. I've changed your life . . . Would it bother you so much to return the favor?

A Great-Grandmother from *Days of Saints*

MATT DI CINTIO

VALENTINE, a man with an offbeat sense of humor, claims to be blind and to have gotten lost after getting off his bus at the wrong stop. He waits for a ride from his lady friend at the home of a novelist, Thomas, who himself waits for his wife. Val stands with a glass.

VAL: I'm going to be a rich man one day. What do you think about that? No, nobody answers when someone announces something like that so certainly, so firmly, so . . . American. My great-grandmother is still alive, do you know that my great-grandmother is still alive?—I'm still talking about scotch, whiskey. Don't think I'm one of those crazies who just keeps changing topics in the middle of a conversation. I can have a full out, real conversation, I have clarity of thought, mental vision, I'm still talking about whiskey. My great-grandmother Alice, she is great, and she is still alive. Whenever we ask Alice about her youth, and we make her speak of it often, there is one year we can't account for. We've figured out it was 1926. Prohibition. Alice calls it The Big Joke. Best we can figure is Alice was doing a little time for bootlegging. She would never admit it, she'd never tell anyone she bootlegged. Or that she still does. Full time. She doesn't consider it very dignified for ladies to speak of how they pass their time. And she keeps very busy. She even sells it to the county sheriff. She's sold it to every county sheriff since the start of Prohibition. Except for one, and he wasn't sheriff for long! There's a shed behind Alice's house, the same house she's lived in since man made fire, but she won't let anybody go into the shed. My mother told me she went in once on a visit, when she was little, very little; she got a beating for it.

And the poor little girl didn't even see what she wasn't supposed to see. Alice sent her out to the back field and made her pick a switch. Alice was always making people pick a switch. If they came back with one that was too skinny, she'd go out front to the magnolia and tear off a branch. Sometimes she made all the children, her own, her children's, their children's, pick switches when others were going to get beat. She made them all pick switches. I think Alice liked to beat people. Likes to beat people. I've had a beating from Alice, just once. It was for spilling paint, and it was, well, ferocious. The way she wielded the branch, and smiled . . . On my twenty-first birthday, Alice took me aside and told me when she dies, I have to go into her bra drawer, and find something she's left for me there. I'm betting it's money. I'm betting she's sewn a whole lot of liquor money into one of her old bras. Money she's saved up since Prohibition until now and forever and who knows how long she's going to keep kicking. A whole fortune laying in there with her skivvies. I'm going to be a rich man one day, and all I have to do is wait for her to die. To Alice!

How I Turned into a Dog from *StudPuppy*

MATTHEW A. EVERETT

SPENCER is working his way through college by walking the local mall in a dog outfit, based on a popular cartoon character. Over the course of the speech, he pulls on the suit, turning from young man into dog.

So here's the story of how I turned into a dog.
Yeah, that's me under there. Or it will be.
So, how I turned into a dog.
I told my parents I was gay.
"Not under my roof, young man."
So I got out from under their roof as often as possible.
We'll pass over my level of popularity with certain members of the track and wrestling teams for the moment, because, hey, this is all about not playing into stereotypes, right? Skip "who," move on to "where"—public parks, restrooms and changing rooms at the local mall, and once, even the back room of a pet store.
No, that's not how.
But, for the record, animals like to watch.
The 'rents did a fine job of avoiding the subject and I did a fair job of not rubbing their faces in it throughout my waning years in high school. Then came time for college. My dad wasn't particularly interested in paying for another roof over my head that he had little or no control over.
I wasn't particularly interested in lying to him or my mother anymore: "Yes, I'm going to college, in part, to become an adult. A gay adult."
Dad said he wasn't going to pay for it.
Mom said nothing.

So I said I'd pay for it.

I spent the rest of the summer sleeping in my friend Jeremy's basement. His parents are bleeding heart liberals who like to have something to show off at parties. I was "Exhibit A" at their Fourth of July cookout.

FYI—Jeremy's cousin Bink is a good kisser, if you ever get out that way. And I'm sure he doesn't always taste like barbecue sauce.

So I pretty much did anything to earn money. Almost anything. Waiting tables, mowing lawns, baby-sitting.

Yes, they trusted me with children.

I got accepted by a number of fine institutions of higher learning. I chose the one as far away from home as I could get.

I don't miss my parents.

Really.

I call home when I have the money. And sometimes when I don't. Mom accepts the charges if she answers. Dad hangs up.

It's just homesickness.

I'll get over it.

(Spencer puts on the dog head. His transformation is complete.)

The Men Who Loved Horse Trailers

DIANE GLANCY

WATKINS, a mixed-blood man who talks about the rodeo. Setting: The part of Texas that is rodeo.

WATKINS: We thought we'd kidnap a horse, ride him bull dogging, which has nothing to do with bulls, but pulling a running steer to the ground. You do this by riding after the steer on your horse and leaning to the side until you have him by the horns and with your weight pull him down. Sometimes you miss and the steer keeps running and you are on the ground with nothing in your hands.

That's why bull dogging is like the rest of your life.

Then we'd take the horse back to the pasture.

There was a girl I wanted. I went after her, jumped from my horse, and went down empty.

It was supposed to be a joke. Take a horse from a pasture. Paint a spot on his nose. Show up at the rodeo with a horse.

The girl I liked in school was shy and none of my friends noticed her. Her name was Nalene. I liked her though. She had a western jean dress with yellow buttons. I got close enough to see the buttons were shaped like horses' heads.

But put it aside. She wouldn't look at me.

We thought we'd just rope a horse and ride him in the pasture. Hank had this horse trailer. So we roped the horse and rode him and put him in the trailer. We drove off not meaning to—but we bull dogged with another man's horse.

What happened?

The horse didn't know what to do. We looked like fools.

Another time, a horse was tied up at a horse trailer behind the arena. We untied him, put another saddle on him. That's Frank Hill's horse, Jake warned. One of the ranchers.

I looked up. There was the shy girl, Nalene, I wanted to be with. Behind her a man stood with folded arms. It was Frank Hill, her father. I knew her last name was Hill, but I didn't know she was *that* Hill. He saw me looking at her. Not in your dreams, he said. She can do what she wants, can't she? Jake pulled me past.

I had saddled the girl's father's horse. That night he stood at the gate as I left.

Not in your dreams.

Not in my dreams, what? What are dreams? Something you can never hold.

A girl who stayed shy as the wind.

The wind ain't shy around here. I been nearly blown from my horse.

For boys, it's all bravery. You can't let your feelings show.

The girls cluster like bees. They keep their little honey hive to themselves.

I been held together with duct tape.

Frank Hill was right. I didn't have a chance.

Rodeo is something that fills the weekend.

It gave us purpose. I'd come home from work on Friday nights and we had something to do. There was excitement. I wasn't tired like I was the other nights. After supper, I'd hook the horse trailer to the truck, load up Zeke, me and my wife would drive off. The dust and the sun going down. The road open under the evening sky. Then in the distance the rodeo. Lights. Trucks and horse trailers. Our rodeo friends. The horses.

For me it was the girls in their jeans and shirts. The calves and the little kids chasing them. The buckaroos. Calf roping. Saddle bronc. Bareback riding. Team roping. Bull dogging. Your wife watching you. It mattered. Sometimes she was talking to the other wives.

There were steers who hated it. Who were scared. There were steers who loved the rodeo. Who could twist at the moment you leaned from the horse and your hands would slip from their heads. They'd trot off to the gate at the end of the arena. Did the steers talk together? Did they know the cowboys who were duds? Did they speak to the horses?

I could never ride broncs or bulls. None of my friends did after once or twice. We were drawn to other things. Bull dogging. Calf roping. It was something we could do without risking the rest of our lives.

I still walk stiff when it rains—or when I'm carrying a bale of hay.

Put Rudy up to something we wouldn't do ourselves. He only wanted to be part of our group. We said he could if he started as a bull rider—same as us. It could happen to anyone.

Our group was never as *groupy* after that.

We had seen something and we didn't know what to do about it. No one had ever said this is what to do. We didn't have answers. We shied away from one another.

We moved on.

Where is she now?

I haven't been back to Corsicana.

I remember Nalene Hill had a skirt with Indians and cowboys on it. Red, turquoise, rust brown. I sat behind her in school. Once I called her name. She looked down. I saw the collar on her shirt when she bowed her head. It had a serrated edge. It was so small I hardly noticed. Maybe her mother or grandmother had made it for her. Maybe they ordered it from a western catalog.

Dreams are horses. A girl's horse is her dream of being a man. Of having her own power. A horse prepares a girl to be a mother. I saw that in my sister.

My floor plan is a horse trailer. Wood floor. Shelf for hay over the tongue of the trailer. The part where it hooks onto the truck.

You can sleep in a horse trailer with your horse tied under the tree.

You're wasting your prize money.
That's what that kind of money is for.
Letting it go.
The night Rudy was killed. He was bull riding. Not many die that way.

Look at Rudy. Trampled to death. Nothing anybody could do. The bull gored him in the back. Right along the spine.

I thought of her horse buttons.
Let her go.
You let go.

Frank Hill won't let you near his daughter, Jake said.
The rodeo ain't everything.
A rodeo is the universe. Most of it anyway.

Later we sank to stealing horse trailers, repainting them in Jake's shed. I worked two jobs to pay the fines when we got caught. We were branded outlaws. Outcasts. We were shunned on the circuit. I rode whatever voice there was to tell me. I rode whatever voice told me to ride.

Face up to the failure. I still like the ride. I got my own horse. I kept him in the yard with no place to run until he stiffened and couldn't extend once I found him a bigger place.

We just got in there and went wild for a while. Our stealing horse trailers was losin' it. Hurtin' people. That's what we did.

The way a child lets his body go limp when he doesn't want to go where you want him to. I know the sound of cries that are protest. They are in my head.

And the wifeandmother dothisdothatwherehaveyoubeen?
The dishwasher drowning the plates and saucers; a plastic cup or something flailing loose.

I carried oats to him in an aluminum bucket.

I tried to find an Indian rodeo outside of the rodeo. The *valiantry* of it.
To rodeo is to be a ranger of the sky.

The horses pulled our wagons west. They carried the cavalry. They carried the ones running from the cavalry, except those at the last running on foot, trying to flee. Black Kettle Grasslands. Wounded Knee.

Now the horses ride.

After Rudy died, I could hear the houses walking.

Those nights at the rodeo glistened like the sun on spider webs in the corner of the barn and between fence rails.

Excerpt from *Day of the Kings*

DAPHNE GREAVES

The sound of distant drumming is heard. Lights up on ESTEBAN, *a seventeen-year-old slave in the household of a rich plantation owner in Cuba in 1820. It is the festival of the Day of the Kings, a time when everyone celebrates by drinking rum and dancing in the streets.*

ESTEBAN: Today is the Day of the Kings and all Havana is celebrating. I too celebrate. But not this lie, this fantasy of all Cubanos free and joyous. For no one in Cuba is free. Not the whites who daily sell their souls to the Spanish Satan and certainly not the black slave who one day a year drinks himself into oblivion that he may sustain the belief—if only for a moment—that his life is his own. No one in Cuba is free. And as for joy, Cubanos have long confused it with hysteria. I do not celebrate a day of kings. I celebrate the birth of a man. *(Indicating himself)* This man. For today is my birthday. Two years ago my mother died and her death gave me a new life by moving the heart of my young mistress to teach me to read. My first written word was my mother's name. Cara, dear one. I devoured her name and have gorged myself since. Words are a meal I can never get enough of. At first I nibbled on almanacs and newspapers but as my appetite grew I raided the family library. I'm sure the master ordered it *prix fixe* for many courses in it his sensitive stomach would find indigestible. But I have feasted on the words of the American Patriot, Thomas Paine— *Aristocracy is a monster founded in the base idea of man having property in man. It degenerates the human spirit*—I have drunk in the philosophy of Jean Jacques Rousseau—*The unconquerable spirit of liberty is man's characteristic*—And I have savored the sweet, sweet poetry of José María Heredia—*Fair land of Cuba!*

On thy shores are seen, life's far extremes of noble and of mean. Hear Cuba the tyrants' clamor, and the slaves' sad cry, with the sharp lash in insolent reply. Cubanos rise, and to power a daring heart oppose! We, too, can leave a glory and a name our children's children shall not blush to claim—On these words I have fed and grown strong. My eyes have opened and now the entire world is my book. I know I am not alone. There are men right here in Havana who think as I do. Desire freedom as I do. Are willing to die for it as I am. From the day I was a tiny boy my mother pushed to get me off the plantation and into the master's house. Paraded me before the master and his mistress—My boy he is so good. So smart. So quick. He will serve you—She said anything to save me from a life of unendurable endless toil and pain in the fields. A mother will say anything to save her child. My mother saved me, *(Raising his fist)* and in her name I will work to save every other mother's child.

(Drums crescendo loudly.)

Excerpt from *Burial at Sea*

IRVING A. GREENFIELD

STEVE WARREN is busy writing at the desk in his study. A desk lamp illuminates him. The remainder of the stage is dark.

STEVE *(leans back and stretches)*: Done! The fucking letter to my sister is done.

(He turns to the audience, and holding the letter in his hand, he stands.)

Roslyn. The letter is for her.

(Beat)

She wanted closure. My—our—other sister, Silvia, died ten days ago. She was nine years older than I and eight years older than Roslyn.

(Beat)

Roslyn was all tears when I called and told her about it.

(Laughs harshly)

She saw her twice in eleven years and those two times were at the nursing home when Silvia didn't know who she was or where she was.

(Beat)

But Roslyn wanted closure. She even put an obit in the local paper where she lives and asked me if I had done the same.

(Beat)

I hadn't. My sister's death means nothing to anyone with the exception of me and Roslyn.

(Beat)

But Roslyn wanted closure. That's what this letter is about—CLOSURE. Silvia was cremated and I buried her at sea.

(He takes several steps to the right and left before stopping.)

The day is cloudy with little wind. I'm in a small white sloop that's owned by a friend of mine, James Sanders.

(Beat)

He asks me about my sister. I answer as objectively as I can. Her life was sadly meaningless. She accomplished nothing. Left nothing. All that remains of her are the ashes in the container next to me.

(Beat)

James heaves to when we are between the Great Kills Harbor and the Jersey shore, about three hundred yards past the first light house.

(Beat)

I slice open the box in which the container was mailed to the funeral home. Inside is a certificate of cremation. For some inexplicable reason, I find that humorous. Perhaps it's the tension of the moment?

(Beat)

Inside the first box there is another box, dark red. It holds the ashes. It is tightly sealed and decorated with a gold star. I cut the star and try to pry open the lid. I even use a screwdriver that I brought along for just such a contingency. I can't open it. To do more with the screwdriver than I already did would require more violence than I want to use. I put the screwdriver down and began to fiddle with the top of the box. By accident, since I have no idea how it happens, I manage to pop the box open.

(Beat)

I nod to James and work my way forward. I reach in and pull out a plastic bag with what looks like grated parmesan cheese in it. The bag is sealed with a white plastic strip pulled tight through a small white locking device that cinches the neck of the bag.

(He moves again before continuing.)

I put the red container down on the deck between my feet and hold the bag. Those ashes that look so much like cheese are all that is left of our sister. There is nothing more. Once those ashes are gone everything physical about her will be gone. She will exist only in our memories and when we're gone, she will be gone.

(Beat)

The relationship between the three of us has been less than satisfactory. But this is not unique in a family.

(Beat)

I try to undo the plastic lock but quickly find I can't. I momentarily thought about slicing the bag open. I want to scatter the ashes over the surface of the water, which reflects the dark gray of the cloud-filled sky. But the idea of sticking a knife into the bag seems to me to be a violation of—

(Beat)

I truly don't know what I'd be violating. But whatever it is, it prevents me from using my knife.

(Beat)

I hold the bag of ashes aware of some kind of emptiness inside of me that feels as if it extends for some distance outside of me. I am also aware of the silence. James is about twenty feet aft of me. The boat rocks with the movement of the water. The sense of being alone is enormous. But the loneliness is neither mournful nor threatening. I'm glad that I'm alone, that there is no one to put an arm around my shoulders and try and console me.

(Beat)

I'm here with my sister's ashes.

(Beat)

I let the bag slip out of my hands. It makes a plopping sound when it crashes through the surface of the water and then it's gone.

(Beat)

I look at the spot where it vanished and remember that as a young woman my sister was a superb swimmer; and I also remember that in the hospital where she died the attending physician and the nurses thought she was my mother.

(Beat)

Those are odd things to think about at this moment. But then my mind seems to go blank.

(Beat)

I sigh deeply and stand up. I was sitting on the forward hatch cover. I steady myself and make my way aft along the narrow walkway to the boat's cockpit.

(Beat)

James asks if I'm all right. "Yes," I answer, "Let's get under way."

(Beat)

The engine coughs a few times then it steadies down to a healthy purr.

(Beat)

It feels colder now than it had before. For a few moments neither of us speak. Then, I thank James and we begin to speak about the everyday things that make up our lives.

(Beat)

We decide to go to the Colonnade Diner on Hylan Boulevard for lunch. It will not be a funeral feast. But in a way it will be, at least that's the way I'll remember it.

(Suddenly he crumples the letter and tosses it into the waste paper basket.)

That was my closure. Yours was a death notice in the newspaper.

Dad and Joey and Ma and Me from *Memories of Childhood*

JUNE GURALNICK

"ME" is a teenage ex-con.

ME: I just left. Think it was spring. I'd cut school to get high and hang out. Dropped by the movies that afternoon to see some Kung Fu flick. *(Laughing)* Chop, chop, chop. After the movie, instead of going home, I drove straight out of town— opposite direction. Called 'em from a fast food place in Iowa City. "I won't be home for dinner . . . don't wait," I said. And then I hung up. Didn't write or call for five years.

Got out of the joint a year ago. Have a regular gig now— cookin' at Jimmy's. Done a pretty good job, too. People actually come in to eat my burgers and fries.

Called the folks the other day. I was flippin' a shake and as the milk bubbled over, I wondered, "How are they?" It took a minute before Ma recognized my voice. There was this pause. I didn't know what to say. So I hung up.

Yeah. Five years since I left. I should miss them but I don't. I miss the idea of them. I watch *Little House on the Prairie*, too. But we weren't like that—my family. I don't know how we were. But we weren't like that.

There's a picture in our living room of the four of us. We're at a barbecue by a lake somewhere or other. Dad is stoking the fire . . . Joey is eating a hot dog—in the picture he's got his mouth wide open and the dog is stuck half-way in. Ma is folding napkins and taking out paper plates—and I'm lookin' straight at the camera. Straight at it. With my tongue out. Like this. *(Sticks tongue out)*

Dad and Joey and Ma and Me. I didn't know them. Any of 'em. Dad and Joey and Ma and Me. Sounds like a rhyme, doesn't it? Dad and Joey and Ma and Me . . . we all lived in separate countries . . . Dad in Africa, Ma in Spain, Joey in Antarctica, and Me in pain . . . Me in pain . . . *(Pause)*

Five years from now, I wonder if they'll recognize my voice?

Excerpt from *Queen Darlene,*
an uncertain valentine

JORDAN HARRISON

VIC WATTS is a record producer in the 1960s. He wears aviator glasses indoors and swivels in a black leather swivel chair. His hi-fi is needling Wagner's Götterdammerung, *faintly. This is his first meeting with Doris, a schoolgirl he will make into a star.*

MR. WATTS: No no no. Doris Unsworth is no *good*. Doris Unsworth doesn't *sing*. What the public wants is Doris DuPont, Doris Dalloway. Doris Delirious, Doris Deleterious, Delicious Doris, Doo-Wop Doris, the Duchess of Doris. Doris Duke. Doris *Day*. All the good ideas in this world are used up. Doris Duvall? Doris DuPont. The public wants alliteration and by God we'll give it to them.
    Or do away with plain ol' Doris all together . . .

(Doris: I don't know if Grandmother would—)

    . . . and we get something like Darlene. *Darlene* DuPont. Darlene DuPont is a girl other girls want to *be*. Done. Then, the question of your sound your unique Darlene voice your *sound*. It's not in the material, it's in the heavy artillery. Reinforcements. Give me a hundred violins, Barry. Give me a millionteen tubas. Electric harpsichords. Marimbas. A chorus of castratos. Castrati? A little combo of Romanian gypsies, for the bridge. Get those gypsies on a plane and bring them here, now. I want a wall of sound for our girl Darlene. I want ears bleeding. I want hearts bleeding. I want little teenage hearts hemorrhaging into the radio, across our great nation. I want some coffee. Somebody get my coffee. Where's the girl with my coffee?
    (Pause)
    You're turning a funny color, Darlene. Barry, get her some powder. The public wants a girl with an even tone.

The Murderer

JEFFREY HATCHER

GERALD HALVERSON, a dapper man in his late thirties, early forties wears a beautifully cut black tuxedo.

GERALD: I am a murderer.

This is my uniform.

All the best murderers wear black tie when committing murder. *Sleuth. Dial "M" for Murder.* Various episodes of *Columbo.* Murder mysteries teach us that. Murder mysteries also teach us that the best murderers always make a fatal mistake. The unforeseen circumstance. The overlooked detail. The character flaw that unravels the whole, perfect, orchestrated plot.

Spiff used to say one should always wear black tie for formal occasions. I should think a murder would qualify.

None of us had any inkling of Spiffy's illness until well after the party for Puss and Peppar. Puss and Spiffy had known each other since they were three years old, and Puss's new husband, Peppar, a "character," a plaid cummerbund, lampshades at parties type who'd been married and widowed twice already, was now taking his new bride away, from the snows of Lake Forest to the shores of Florida.

The farewell party is marvelous! That's one of Spiff's words: marvelous! A debutante's word from the forties. Spiff was one of those "gals" who studied *Vogue* for a living and never settled for that aging Vassar-hairband look. Spiff is a widow herself. Her husband died fifteen years ago. Tonight she is wearing one of her Ultra-Suede pantsuits with the Nehru tunic and military buttons. She looks like Diana Vreeland's idea of "Dr. No."

Ting ting ting ting! Spiff is making a toast.

"Those of you who can still raise your arms above your chests, please take up a glass. It is hard to find one love of your life, let alone a second. Puss, you and Peppar are truly blessed. Bon voyage!"

Hear, hear, clink-clink. Drink.

The next day Puss and Peppar flew down to Florida. Three weeks later Puss was dead.

She'd gotten a cold that turned into pneumonia and then her respirator gave out.

Peppar called Spiff with the news: "Puss was in such pain. It was better this way. I'm gonna move to Arizona."

Spiff took Puss's death well and didn't want to discuss the details. She hates anything to do with doctors, hospitals. She had to be in a convalescence home once for a week when she'd pulled the tendons in her hip. She kept moaning, "Just let me go."

It was a hip sprain.

When people die, Spiff takes it, marks it, and moves on.

Laura takes a dim view of this. "Mom has never shown much emotion about anyone's death. I think that's horrible."

Laura thinks one should work harder to get to the grief that you then have to work harder to get out of.

Spiff never knows what to call me: son-in-law, daughter's boyfriend, live-in lover . . .

Laura and I are not married. We met fifteen years ago in college outside Washington, D.C., in West Virginia of all places, lived there together for seven years, so I joke with Spiff, that we're probably a common-law couple anyway. Spiff loves us, but our unmarried status irritates her. It's impractical. And she is nothing if not a highly practical woman. As you shall see.

The first inkling of her illness came in February. Her appetite was poor. She had been tired a lot. Laura took her to Dr. Rosenblum for some tests. A few days later, he called and said we should all come in.

"Spiff. It's your kidneys. You have ninety percent failure. You have six, eight weeks at the most."

As we left the office, Spiff marches to the elevator and presses the up button.

Laura looks at me, "Mom, we're going down, not up."

Spiff snaps: "Up is where my lawyers are."

She had made the appointment in advance.

In the lawyer's office, we sit down with the estates attorney, Arthur Adelot, which sounds like a mnemonic, but is actually his name. Arthur is a man whose discretion is so discreet it is not even noticed.

Adelot is holding a print-out.

"Your estate, as of this morning, is estimated at approximately five million dollars, give or take."

Spiff nods. "And what happens to it if I die today?"

"Weel, your heir is your daughter, Laura, and her . . . boyfriend, yes? Weel, the Feds, for your bracket, take forty percent. Forty percent of five million is two million, leaving three million."

Spiff nods. "Three million. Not bad."

"Weel, it's not so simple as that. You see, you don't have the two million in cash. You'd have to sell stock. Your stocks are very old. Heirs will have to pay capital gains. That's another third. Now you're down to two million. Sell the house, there's more capital gain, now you're under one million five."

Spiffy gives us a dirty look: "All those years you kept trying to make me vote Democratic. Isn't there any way around this goddamn mess!?"

This is the first emotion I have seen Spiffy reveal so far. And it has not been about her pending death. It is about her pending death tax.

Adelot shakes his head: "The only sheltered arrangement the Feds recognize is that between a husband and his wife. A spouse may leave any amount to the remaining spouse, and the IRS can't touch a penny of it."

Now, I cannot tell you that it was much later that the plan struck me . . .

. . . because it struck me immediately.

The only question was: how to bring it up.

That night, over dinner at the club, I gin up my courage to speak when Spiff suddenly looks across the table and says:

"I think we should get married."

Laura looks up. Who?

"Arthur said a spouse could leave any amount to the remaining spouse without paying a penny in taxes. I think Gerald and I should get married, so that when I die, you two can inherit my estate without having to pay the goddamn government. I have two months. That's plenty of time to . . . do all the official things, and then . . . when I'm gone . . . you two get everything."

There is a requisite stunned silence. Laura is actually stunned, I'm requisite.

Spiff goes on.

"Now, we couldn't get married here. I wouldn't want anyone to know. Not for my sake, I'm going to be dead, but for Laura's."

Laura sputters. "Mother, this is ridiculous! My husband is not marrying my mother."

"Honey, he's not your husband. You know I think Gerald is marvelous, but he's never going to make much money. Nor will you. You've practically been living off me for years! You need something solid to rest on!"

Spiff actually likes me a lot, but she is not blind to the fact that I'm a ne'er do well who's never going to keep her daughter in the manner to which Spiff thinks she should be accustomed.

I am aching to turn to Laura and say, "She's right, you know." After all, Spiff has come up with the same plan as I. But the best thing is for Laura to come to the decision by herself, on her own.

It comes that night. After the drive home in our Toyota, as we pass the BMWs and the Jaguars driven by people far less deserving, interesting, and ironic as we. It comes at the apartment that night. The is it funky? Are we bohemian? Aren't we a little old for this kind of life? apartment we've been living in for ten years; when we're holding close under the covers, without a word until Laura says, "Where would you have to go to get married?"

Florida. The Riddle Key Condominium Community.

Riddle Key is one of those upscale, gated, waterfront developments that caters to "seasoned citizens." "Seasoned." Like we're going to eat them. For five hundred thousand dollars, Riddle Key provides you with a two bedroom luxury condo with a five year lease. You're betting you don't die before year five or after year five. They're betting you die . . . well, they're just betting you die. A surprising number of people die on the fifth anniversary exactly. The greatest generation is nothing if not prompt.

Dr. Rosenblum has given Spiff a month, two at the outset. After we arrive in Florida and marry at a Justice of the Peace, we settle in and wait it out. I keep a diary with notes and observations:

Week One. I did not know Bob Barker's hair was white. I am not usually up by eleven most days, but now eleven is lunch time. Call Laura every day. Dinners are pretty basic. Lean Cuisines mostly. Note to self: Brillo pads cost more than I would have guessed.

Week Two. *The Young and the Restless* is actually a pretty good show. No sign yet of physical deterioration in Spiff. Call Laura every other day. She has moved from our apartment into Spiff's house. Which surprises me. But it is practical. Went out to dinner once this week. Everyone eats at 5 P.M. and goes to bed before sundown. It's like living at the Antarctic.

Week Three: Naps are good. Spiff holding up well, so went to dinner three times this week and out to lunch twice. Talked to Laura Sunday. She's bought a new car. A Jaguar with a voice activated phone and satellite directional system. Laura is getting used to her new status.

Week Four: A knock at the door.

This is the first this has happened. Spiff and I look at each other as if G-Men have come to arrest us.

When I open the door I see standing on the threshold a strange mirror image of ourselves. An old woman, like Spiff but older, and a man, like me but . . . weirder. She's a blue rinse number in a lavender silk pantsuit with lots of jewelry. He's in his fifties, but his hair is blonde, Rumplestiltskin gold.

"Hi. Jerry Waldenow."

"And I'm Shirl. We live in the condo across the street, seen you come in and out. We're going to dinner. Would you like to join us?"

I am about to politely decline, when I hear Spiff say:

"That would be marvelous."

We go to dinner at the Blue Hair Café, which is the first evidence I've seen of irony in Florida. Shirl is eighty-seven years old, formerly of Riverdale in the Bronx. Husband Irving was very successful in the flooring business. He died three years ago soon after they came down to Riddle Key.

Shirl sniffs, takes Jerry's hand. "I met Jerry on a cruise. And it's been bliss ever since."

Jerry is more than thirty years younger than Shirl. With his double breasted blue blazer and orange ascot, he looks like a kid's version of a sophisticate, circa 1973. I don't think he is with Shirl or indeed any woman for "the physical part," though I get the idea from Shirl's comments that he "performs well." Shirl is open about such things.

Spiff is open about her illness, about how long she's got. Shirl and Jerry are very sympathetic. When the evening is over and we're back at Riddle Key—Shirl calling out so all the burglars can hear, "Visit anytime, the garage door's always open!"— I say to Spiff: "Can you believe it? He's a gigolo."

Spiff surprises me.

"Oh, who cares if he's a gigolo? He doesn't have to be with an eighty-seven-year-old woman. I'm sure he could be with a seventy-seven-year-old woman. It's money well spent."

"So you grant he's only in it for the money."

"Unlike . . . ?"

I start to stammer, unable to defend myself without sounding pompous and sputtering, like I'm Mr. Mooney.

Spiff rescues me. She pats my cheek.

"Don't get all worked up. Our children get so righteous when it comes to sex and money."

And she goes into her bedroom.

Week Six. Spiff is gaining weight. She'd lost fifteen pounds up north, but now she's gaining. Her Doctor No outfits don't fit anymore. I suggest we see a physician.

Spiff says, "Isn't my dying the whole idea?"

She has a point, but I convince her to make an appointment with the onsite physician, Dr. Nagangupta. We have had her medical records sent from Lake Forest.

Says Dr. Nagangupta: "I would like to run a few tests of my own."

Spiff relents. Dr. Naganupta will let us know the results.

As we leave the office we see Shirl and Jerry pull up in a 1965 red convertible Mustang. Would we like to join them for nine holes?

Jerry says: "You gotta work on your tan, Ger."

I realize suddenly we have the same name. Gerald and Jerry. He's my gay, suntanned gigolo doppelganger.

I start to politely decline when I hear:

"That would be marvelous!"

Nine holes. Which for someone like me is like the opening of *Saving Private Ryan*.

Spiff and Shirl tease me about my gasping, my sweating, my calling for medics.

At that precise moment a voice calls out: "SPIFF!"

We turn from the hole to see a small, wizened man has made his way to the putting green.

"Peppar! What the hell are you doing here?"

Peppar toddles up in his golf togs. "I came back. I did not like all the young people in Arizona."

Peppar looks at me. He can't place me. I'm out of context.

Spiff stumbles through the introductions. "Peppar, this is Shirley, Jerry, and this is my . . . this is Gerald, you remember you met him at the party for you and Puss."

Peppar has tears in his eyes.

"Y'know, Spiff . . . Puss was in such pain. It was good she went like she did. So much pain. My first two wives, too." There is a moment of silence. Then Peppar claps his hands. "Hey. Spiff. How about we cut the rug? There's a Swing Dance at the club Saturday night! We could all go! You, me, Shirl, and Jerry!"

I have been left out.

Jerry leaps in. "What about Gerald?"

Peppar squints at me. "You wanna come with us old folk? Wouldn't you rather be off at one of your protest meetings or hootenannies?"

Spiff takes my hand. "You've been cooped up with me for weeks. Besides, it's a formal affair, and you don't own a dinner jacket. Take Saturday night off, have a night on the town."

Peppar says, "Yeah, you can go hang out with your Smothers Brothers and your Timothy Learys."

When we get back to the condo, the fight commences.

"I don't want you going out with Peppar!"

"What do you think is going to happen? Peppar's almost ninety. The last time we ate together I had to cut his meat."

"How would you feel if I went out on a date?"

"I don't think someone would like that."

"Ha. I didn't think you would."

"I mean: Laura."

There is no possible response I can make that will salvage me. But Spiff does. She comes to me, puts a hand on my cheek, smiling, forgiving whatever sin there is.

I stare into her eyes.

I see her at her debut, at a dance fifty years ago. In the back of a car, in a rumble seat, bathtub gin and a cigarette in the wind. The smell of lilacs breezing over a country club veranda as she closes her eyes and tilts back her head for her first kiss.

I lean towards Spiff. The tiniest movement.

She turns.

She goes off to her bedroom and flicks on the TV. *Murder She Wrote* is on.

This is Monday night. The dance is Saturday. The next days' Diary entries go like this:

Tuesday: Spiff goes to a dress shop and buys what I would consider a very revealing black dress.

Wednesday: Spiff gets a hairdo, a manicure, and a pedicure.

Thursday: Spiff buys a pair of evening shoes. The shoes are not open toed. So, I ask you: What was the pedicure for? At what point in the evening does she intend to be wearing no shoes AND showing her toes?

That afternoon I go out to take a walk along the docks and look at the ocean. As I pass the clinic, Dr. Nagangupta waves me inside.

"I have back your wife's tests."

I nod, "Doctor, we know the diag—"

"The diagnosis you had is very wrong. It is in fact completely incorrect. Where your Doctor Rosenblum has her with ninety percent kidney failure, he has misread the chart. It is nineteen percent kidney failure."

"But what about the weakness? The sleeping?"

"Oh, she has kidney trouble, yes, but it can be addressed through dialysis along with diet and medication."

"But her gaining weight. Isn't that bad?"

"No! Her appetite is back. We have many fine restaurants in Riddle Key. I tell you this first because I think good news should come from loved ones. Don't you?"

"Doctor, what will happen if she doesn't receive treatment, dialysis?"

"Well . . . you must start dialysis immediately . . . without that . . . a month, maybe, two . . . she'll die."

I started back to the condo.

I tried to think.

I should tell Spiff immediately, tell her the good news.

Instead I call Laura from the clubhouse payphone.

Laura does not answer. The architect answers. He's doing drawings for the new addition. Laura has gone away for the weekend. To a spa.

Says the architect: "Oop. Gotta go. Pool contractor's here."

So I do not tell Spiff the news. I do not tell her that night. Or the next morning or the next day or the day after that.

Dr. Nagangupta said she could live no more than two months without treatment. Years with. But surely a day or two's delay won't hurt.

On the third day, Saturday, I wake early and head down to the shore to take a walk, clear my head, when Jerry's red Mustang comes into view. He is alone.

"Gerald! Got a minute?"

He gets out of the car and we stand at the edge of the ocean.

"Shirl slipped in the garage last night. Broke her hip. They did an X-ray. Bone cancer. Terminal. She's in the hospital now. Hey. Guess I'll have to go to the dance alone tonight. But seriously, Ger, that's not what I wanted to talk to you about. See, it was Dr. Nagangupta who treated her. He said, "I wish it was good news I was telling you . . . like Mr. Halverson."

I swallow.

"Have you told Spiff her good news?"

I hesitated.

"You're hesitating. You're thinking of lying to me. I've just been chatting with Spiff in the backyard and she reiterated that she only has a matter of weeks. You know what I think? I think Gerald's being a naughty gigolo. I think Gerald's hoping Spiff kicks it sooner rather than later. Am I right?"

"What do you want?"

"Half of everything you'll get. You can start now. Ten thousand a month."

"What if I go right back to the condo right now and tell Spiff the truth?"

"Three days late? I get Nagangupta to tell Spiff that he told you the good news three days ago Spiff's gonna wonder why her loving husband waited three days to tell her."

I look like I'm trying to decide. Then I sigh.

"Ten thousand. I'll give you a check tonight. After the dance."

"Goody. Ciao, fella!"

His convertible zooms away, the exhaust fumes trailing his wake.

It would have to be that night. The dance begins at 6 P.M.

Ten A.M. When I get back to the condo, Spiff is taking a shower. I go into the utility room and find bleach and ammonia. From the kitchen, I get a large plastic baggie.

Noon. Take a quick trip into Sarasota to a beauty salon to get some supplies. Pay in cash.

One P.M. Stop at a hardware store. Get a large sponge and a pair of yellow rubber gloves. Pay in cash.

Two P.M. Stop at a clothing store and a bookstore. Buy certain essentials for the evening. Cash.

Four P.M. Back at the condo. Spiff is taking her nap. I check the book I've bought for information on toxins and the respiratory system.

Five o'clock. Spiffy is dressed and ready when the doorbell rings.

Peppar is here.

"Hey, fella! Not smokin' any of that ganja reefer, I hope!"

I fix Spiff and Peppar a couple of drinks. I check my watch. 5:43. When I look up Spiff is staring at me.

"Gerald? Why don't you come with us? Peppar wouldn't mind, would you, Pep?"

"No, heck, I don't mind if he comes. Just don't be doin' that boogaloo stuff."

I say: "But I didn't bring dinner clothes. You said one should always wear black tie for formal occasions."

Spiff is gazing at me. She takes my hand. "Sweetie . . . in your case . . . I'd make an exception."

Peppar cuts in. "Don't beg him, Spiff! A punk like him might feel funny without his disco pants and his moccasins."

And so they go.

Before Spiff is out the door, she suddenly comes round and kisses me. Not quite the cheek, not quite the lips. But inside the range of impropriety.

Once Peppar's Lincoln has pulled away, I go into gear.

First to my bedroom to get the new tux I've brought. Spiff hasn't seen it, so that was fairly easy to get away with.

In the bathroom, I comb in the blonde hair color I got at the beauty salon. I look in the mirror. From a distance, it will do.

I turn on my computer and get on the internet, so there will be a record of my alibi. That will also serve to block any incoming calls.

I pour the bleach and the ammonia into the baggie, then let the sponge soak up the concoction. I seal the bag. I get the rubber gloves.

I walk evenly across the street. If anyone sees me, they'll think I'm him. And if anyone asks what he was doing at my house, I'll tell them he came over for a drink. He was despondent.

The garage door is always open, Shirl said. And it is.

There, inside, is the Mustang. Candy red, the white top down.

I hear a sound at the door to the kitchen. I back behind the garbage can and put on the plastic gloves. The door opens and there he is. In a tux. Like mine. Hair like mine. Beard and mustache like mine. I open the baggie.

He gets in behind the wheel. He slips the key into the ignition.

And the sponge goes around his face. His arms flail a moment, I dodge his nails. Then he slumps. Five seconds. The sponge goes back into the baggy.

Inside the condo, I get towels and stuff them under the garage doors.

I take Jerry's fingers, place them on the key and turn the ignition. The V-8 motor roars. And the exhaust pours out of the pipe. A car that vintage with a V-8 engine, he should be dead in twenty minutes.

I leave the way I came.

Once back in the condo, I take the sponge, the rubber gloves and the baggie and melt them all on the patio grill. I wash out my hair and mustache, wash off my face.

And then I wait. I rehearse my speech. I will call Laura. And I will tell her I am not coming back. I will explain as best I can. But I must save my strength and courage and I daresay eloquence . . . for Spiff.

I must tell her about Dr. Nagangupta's diagnosis.

I must convince her of the treatment that will add years to her life.

And I must persuade her to make our marriage real.

I have realized—as far back as the moment Jerry told me he planned to blackmail me—that what I feared was not the loss of five million dollars. It was the loss of her.

It's just past eight when I hear the sirens.

I peek through the front curtains. The sirens are getting closer. I can see the reflection of the red and blue lights in the palm trees.

Then I see the ambulance.

It zooms around the corner, down the street towards Jerry's house.

And then . . . it zooms by.

I watch as the lights go around the curve and up, up the street . . . to the club.

By the time I reach the clubhouse, I see the crowd gathered at the door to the ballroom.

Inside, Peppar kneels on the parquet.

On the floor is Spiff, on her back, an oxygen mask over her face. Medics are working on her . . .

As we rush into the hospital, Peppar tries to explain.

"We were dancing and she was laughing and then she just went down like a sack of tomatoes."

I tell the nurse who I am. "I am her husband."

She tries not to react to this, says they're checking for everything, heart, stroke.

I tell them . . . "Her kidneys are in end stage renal failure."

The nurse asks: "Is she taking medication, on dialysis?"

"No."

She stares at me a beat. "She's not under treatment?"

" . . . No."

The nurse picks up the phone. "Who is your doctor?"

"Our doctor?"

"Sir, who is your doctor and when did your wife last see him?"

I open my mouth to answer . . . but I am saved by Spiff. They're bringing her into ICU on a stretcher. Her face has a grimace on it.

Peppar stands and groans: "She is in such pain."

The nurse says: "She's been asking for her husband."

A rush of warmth comes over me. Then I think:

"Which husband did she ask for?"

I go into the room. The whoosh of the respirator, the beep of the heart monitor crowd my thoughts as the doctors and nurses whisper behind me.

Someone taps my shoulder. A gentleman wants to see you.

I go into the hall. Standing there is a little, bald man with a . . . police badge.

"Sergeant Batista. I am sorry about your wife. Hope everything works out. May I speak to you a moment?"

"Certainly, sergeant."

"There was a death on your street this evening. Mr. Jerry Waldenow?"

"Oh. No."

"Exhaust fumes, very old car. But pretty. I wish I had such a car. I wanted to ask if there was anything that you might have noticed about him recently, anything strange, peculiar . . . ?"

"No. No. Well. Well . . . he did tell me . . . he told me recently . . . actually . . . that his wife was very ill . . . terminal."

"Terminal you say?"

"He seemed . . . despondent."

"Despondent. I see. Well. Of course we have to treat it as any mysterious death. Could have been an accident, he got in

76

the car, turned it on, fell asleep. Or if we find some knock-out drug in his system. Or a bonk on the head, a bruise."

I think to myself: "You won't find drugs and you won't find a bruise."

"Still I bet we come out with suicide. Well, thank you very much, sir. Hope everything works out with your wife."

When Sergeant Batista is gone I go back into the ICU room. Peppar has tottered off somewhere.

It's so quiet in there.

I take her hand. I look at her fingers. The wedding ring her first husband gave her. I never gave her a ring. I'll correct that. I'll get it right this time.

Then I notice something. Why is it so quiet? No whoosh. No beep. Then a sound begins. I look at the monitor next to the bed. The green line, the flat . . . I look down. The plug on the respirator. I go to the floor. I try to stick it back in . . .

That's when the doctors and the nurses rush into the room . . . and see me. On the floor, with the plug in my hand.

Sergeant Batista gets the case.

He speaks to Dr. Nagangupta, Laura, the lawyers, the Justice of the Peace.

I make a show of protest, but I am not convincing, so I am convicted.

First degree murder. Death penalty.

Laura does not speak to me again. Ever.

But her representative does. Arthur Adelot. He has news.

"According to your mother-in-law's new will you are the beneficiary of her entire estate. But since you're about to die . . ."

"Naturally I will leave the entire five million to Laura."

"Weel. It's not that simple. You met Laura in college, yes?"

"Yes."

"Lived in West Virginia for seven years, yes?"

" . . . Yes . . . ?"

"West Virginia has common-law marriage. According to West Virginia law you were legally married. To Laura. So when you attempted to marry her mother in Florida you were committing bigamy, and hence . . . the will is invalid. Which means the estate will go into probate . . . which means years, attorney's fees . . . . money will go through the usual tax, forty percent, capital gains, lose the house. Laura will be lucky to walk away with less than a million. Just thought you should know."

And he left.

I never got another visitor . . . ever . . . except one.

Peppar came to visit. Week before the execution. He wanted to show his sympathy. His fellow feeling.

The fan was blowing in the visitor's room.

He said: "I understand. Spiff was in such pain. It was the same with Puss. And my first two wives. They were in such pain."

And then . . . Peppar leaned down and pulled the plug from the fan.

And he looked at me. And winked.

"We do what we must. Take care, boy." He knocked for the guard and pointed to the TV. "Don't be watchin' too much *Hullabaloo!*"

I suppose I could have contacted a lawyer and told him about Peppar. Hoped for a stay of execution, a new trial . . .

But what's the point, really? I had committed murder, and I was being punished, albeit not for the murder I had committed. Such is the fate of a generation raised on irony.

My last request is to wear black tie.

I tell my keepers: "My wife always said one must wear black tie for formal occasions. I should think an execution would qualify . . . "

It'll probably be an orange jumpsuit.

As I sit here and wait . . . I realize . . . I am no one's boyfriend anymore. No one's son-in-law. No one's husband.

I am a murderer. And that will have to do.

Excerpt from *What Remains*

RYAN HILL

MATT meets his recently-deceased lover's unsympathetic mother for the first time.

MATT: I went to the station. I identified his body. I cried in the morgue. I gave them your number. And you whisked him off. They wouldn't even let me pick up his stuff. I asked where this ring was. They told me only family members could do that. Family members or a spouse. And since I obviously wasn't his wife, I had no right.

Do you know how they got a hold of me? Do you know how I found out? He had my cell phone number in his pocket. He never remembered it, so he kept a little Post-it in his pocket.

They called my number and asked who I was. They told me there was an accident and I needed to come downtown. I saw him, and again they asked who I was. They asked who I was in relationship to Erik. I told them. Do you know what they wrote down? They wrote "friend." They said that I was his friend.

I'm not his friend.

And I'm sorry if you can't come to terms with that. But I need no substantiation.

I'm sorry for what you've gone through. I really am. But my sympathy is limited.

You could be right. This could all be a big mistake. But if you want to talk, we talk now. You've run out of time. I can't wait. None of us can wait anymore. So end this horrible, horrible day of yours if you want. Go back to your hotel room and put it off. Let all this . . . unpleasantness water down. Bury his life like you buried his body. Ignore it all ever happened.

This is his ring. This is my ring. They're identical. Do you understand? Do you get it? We bought these for each other.

Look. This is my ring. This is his ring. You're damn right this means more to me than it does for you. And don't you ever call them cheap.

Excerpt from *Phoenix*

CORY HINKLE

RICHARD: Stories used to be my passion, but now I'm sick of them. I can break down the whole of human history, every god damn story ever told into three different types and I'm peddling these three all over America like a tired salesman in an old beat up Chevy to a bunch of mindless twits who if once in their lives read something other than the stories they've been force fed since birth, if they read something other than a story about a hooker turned wife or a high school reunion where *everybody's changed* or a homely girl who's miraculously transformed into a princess with a little pancake makeup, they'd shit their pants and burn every copy in the school gymnasium. That's why we're leaving New York. We're traveling west to find something *real.* I know it's out there—America. Some little house up on some hill. Couple of goats. Maybe a *monkey.* I don't know. A barbed wire fence! We'll find it. Go out West, get a look at some working-class people. Some miners. Factory workers. Farmers. You know what people like now? Images. We'll go out West with a camera, bring back pictures of real people. Poor dirty sad American people. Kind of people that'll make your heart bleed they're so ignorant. God I'm sick of books and words. Sick. It's all old and boring. I want something real. Dirty. Grimy. Gritty.

Excerpt from *Independency*

MARK STEVEN JENSEN

BENJAMIN FRANKLIN, in his seventies, attempts to woo the widowed French aristocrat, Madame Helvetius, while they play chess.

BENJAMIN: No, no, I played my utmost. That is the way with chess.

New strategies appear with every game. That is why it is so entirely fascinating. Let's play again.

(As they do, Benjamin steals amorous glances at Madame Helvetius.)

Last night I had a dream, Madame Helvetius. I dreamt I was in the Elysian Fields, and I met your late husband. Your husband asked me many things about the war, French politics, liberty. But nothing of you! Can you imagine, here you are so devoted to his memory, but he thinks on you not! Check. So I asked him, what about your friend Madame Helvetius, she still loves you dearly back on earth. And he said he was very fond of you, but now he had taken another wife. Brilliant move, Madame, but I can answer you. See? Now, this is what your husband told me. "My new wife is not so beautiful," he said, "but she has good sense and plenty of wit." When his new wife joined us, I was shocked, because I immediately recognized her as my own dearly departed Madame Franklin. I was indignant and claimed her again, but Deborah said to me, "I was a good wife to you for forty-nine years and four months. Be content with that!" Then she was gone. So you see, our better halves are now whole. As we should be. I wish to marry you, Madame Helvetius. Checkmate.

Excerpt from
A Chat with Him and Her

MARK STEVEN JENSEN

HIM, twenties to sixties, stands near a chair while his landlady plays a Wurlitzer on the floor below. He practices a speech that he plans to say to his brother.

HIM: So tell me, Plato. Why does this woman take pleasure in violating music? She's practicing, you'd answer. But for what purpose, I ask? She's too old to become a serious musician. Why does she bother? Practicing for the betterment of the self, you'd say. Betterment in and of itself, even private betterment, is both noble and just. I need to practice again, too. I should confront him, no, no, I must confront him. Practice. Okay. So practice.

(Angrily confronts chair)

How could you . . . to her again? And don't start your drunken excuses. Tonight is reckoning time. Reckoning time. Look up at me, hey, I said look up at me! Right at my eyes, so I know you are listening, hey, look up at me! I said tonight is reckoning time. Tonight was the last night that you will . . . that you will beat her. You want to know why? Because I'm going to kill you. That's right. You're dead. I've got it all planned out. Bang.

(The Wurlitzer plays a long bad note and continues.)

I'll never say that to him. He certainly wouldn't be scared. He'd just laugh and break my nose. All right, relax, regroup.

(Shakes himself like a boxer)

New tactic, new tactic, new tactic!

(Angrily confronts chair)

I said tonight is reckoning time! Look up at me, I said look up at me. Right into my eyes, so I know that you are listening, hey, look up at me! I'm having her move in with me. She's nearly moved in now. She'll live with me. You'll live away from her. And she'll live with me. Simple. It will solve everything. She'll live with me and you won't live with her!

(Wurlitzer plays.)

Redundancy for emphasis, might be all right. Do you have to maul that damn song!

(He nearly bangs the chair on the floor.)

She'll evict me. She's practicing, you're practicing, let her do her thing. Back up again, big man, retry, back into the prize fight. Fight tactic. Fight! Fight tactic!

(Angrily confronts chair)

I said tonight is reckoning time! Look up at me, I said look up at me, right into my eyes, so I know you are listening, hey, look up at me! I love your wife! I always have. I should be the one who . . . I would be perfect for her, understand! Perfect. Perfect, for her!

(He sits in the chair.)

If I wasn't such a coward I'd actually try one of these tactics on you. Luckily for the three of us, I'm . . . I'm a coward.

(The Wurlitzer plays a long, deep tone, and then continues playing during the blackout.)

Lightning

KEVIN KLING

I'll never forget the time my father and I got hit by lightning. We were working on an airplane, a plane called a Bonanza. My dad always had airplanes when I was growing up. In fact, when I was born, my father was putting wings on a Piper Cub, and when he heard I was being born, he rushed to the hospital with airplane goop and dope dripping from his hands. But the time we got hit by lightning, we were working on a Bonanza.

I was lying in this puddle of water, and my dad had just asked for a screwdriver. So I reached over to get one. It was underneath the airplane in the same puddle of water. I handed him the screwdriver, when this big thunderhead, one of these big thunderheads that we get in Minnesota, went right over my head, and I thought, oh no, we're going to get soaking wet out here, when bam, this bolt of lightning shot through the puddle and hit my body. I felt my organs bonk against each other. I thought, oh god, I've been hit by lightning! I've been hit by lightning!

"Dad, Dad, we've been hit by lightning!"

And he said, "God dammit, that does it, let's go home.

Farm boy. Can't stay out here all day, we'll just keep getting hit by lightning."

A few years ago, my father passed away. I was at his funeral at this large table with my uncles, my brother, and my grandpa. We were talking about my dad, remembering him as vividly as possible because we knew we weren't going to get any new memories. We were holding on to the old ones as tightly as we could. So I decided I would tell them the story about how dad and I got hit by lightning. I started into it, and I had just gotten started when my Uncle Don sitting next to me said, "Wait a second. Wait a second. I've been hit by lightning. I've been hit three times."

He said, "Once you get hit by lightning, your chances of getting hit again increase by over fifty percent."

Then my brother said, "Uh, oh."

He'd been hit by lightning. He'd been hit last summer while pumping gasoline. Then my grandpa says, "I've been hit by lightning." He'd been coming in from the fields with his tool belt on when, BAM, lightning hit right beside him and he went up in the air and formed a fountain with himself and his tools. Then my Uncle Byron suddenly chimed in and said, "Wait a second, I've been hit by lightning." Uncle Byron said he'd been hit four times. Uncle Byron, who has a metal plate in his head from the war. He drives one of these metal Airstream trailers.

We said, "Byron, you're beggin' for it pal."

So I found out right then and there that my uncles, my grandpa, my brother, my dad, and myself had all been hit by lightning. That was the day, as they put it, that I found out I was not adopted.

MD Carnival

KEVIN KLING

When I was a kid, I played baseball in the summers. I batted first in the lineup, standing at the plate, teeth gritting, bubble gum in my cheek and evil in my eye. Mr. Haynes, our coach is yelling, "Good eye Kev, Good eye." Now, "Good eye Kev," was actually code for "Don't swing the bat, Kev." I was tiny, not little, tiny, and no pitcher could throw me a strike. I had no strike zone. I mean, the number on my shirt was tucked into my pants, so if I stood my ground, I walked to first every time. But man, I wanted to hit that ball so bad, because in the stands was my friend Cheryl Ludwig.

Cheryl was my best friend. She was teased a lot for running like a girl, that way of running like Marilyn Monroe, arms out to the side, hips swaying, knees together, feet shooting out in all directions. Cheryl's body was changing. So people, mostly young boys, focused on that, and missed out on how cool and funny she was.

"Good eye Kev. Atta boy," yells Mr. Haynes.

Cheryl knew what I knew. Because of my arm people made immediate assumptions about me. They called my arm withered or crippled, or asked "What happened?" or "You poor thing." By the words they chose, I could tell whether they blamed God, my parents, the world, or themselves for my condition. With that information, I could get what I needed from them. It wasn't purposeful. It wasn't even conscious. It was the way a kid works.

The pitcher tried to get one over. "Good eye Kev, atta boy."

God, I want to swing that bat so bad. I decide the next pitch I'm going to swing no matter what. Even if I miss, it's only one strike.

Cheryl and I had a carnival for muscular dystrophy. We sent away for the packet that told how to have a backyard carnival for your neighborhood, and raise money for this worthy cause. I couldn't wait for the packet to tell us how to turn my ordinary backyard into the greatest show on earth. I would be Jimmy Stewart the jocular clown and Cheryl the rope-spinning butterfly. But when the packet came, the games didn't seem fun at all; some lame ring toss game, a totally unfunny clown kit. I mean it was disappointing like getting sea monkeys all over again.

Cheryl said, "This won't make a dime."

I asked what we should do. She said, "Give them what they want."

So, we made up our own MD carnival. We hung up blankets in the yard to create the big top, and borrowed the mimeograph machine at school to make announcements of the upcoming spectacle. God, those announcements smelled good. On show day, I put on swim fins and a snorkel, stripped to the waist, took off my brace, laid on a table and became . . . "Dolphin Boy." I had to be constantly sponged with a saline solution to keep my skin moist, like it was in my natural habitat, the ocean. To the wonder of the crowd, I performed math problems by means of honking a toy horn. I also pretended to have trouble breathing to add pathos to the situation, and to show I'd rather be swimming free with my own kind. I was a hit. Then Cheryl did an exotic dance she called "Dance of the Seven Veils," revealing mysteries of the Orient, and bringing culture to the unwashed masses. Man o' man, it brought the house down. Word got out. Full houses every show. We could've run forever. We raked in the money for muscular dystrophy, and had enough left over to pay the performers.

"Good eye Kev."

But now the pitcher winds up and throws an obvious ball four. But this time I swing. I swing with all my might, and the ball rolls harmlessly toward shortstop. I run toward first base. The shortstop picks up the ball and heaves it to first. The ball takes a short hop off the first baseman's leg and into the outfield. I scamper to second, and don't even look. I'm going to third, this may never happen again. Our whole team yells, "No!" I know Mr. Haynes is livid. The ball flies past me while I'm not even halfway to third, but it sails way over the third baseman's head. I round third for home. I hit home plate and who is coming toward me. Not Mr. Haynes, oh no, we'll have a talk later. No, it's Cheryl Ludwig, running like a girl.

Excerpt from *Room 214*

CARSON KREITZER

BELLBOY: You wouldn't believe.

The privileged information.

What I've seen. Heard.

Fish-eye distorted, curvature of the reverse peephole the curvature of my universe. Space curved. Time curved. Usually you don't get to see it.

You don't get to see it.

I do.

People wonder why I don't leave this job. I do have that degree from Prestigious Eastern University. No kidding. You couldn't pay me to leave this job.

I see the universe. In here.

It comes to me.

It registers at the front desk. Lightning-fast credit check. Card okay. Come right in.

They don't see me as I pick up their bags. Never do. Paying. They don't have to see.

I am an eyeball. Veins and cavernous spaces. Reflecting. Refracting. Recording. I see their every vice. Their every prayer. Hope and desperation. I can smell it off them. In between the sweat and stale cigar and Yves St. Laurent. Rive Gauche. No one wears that anymore. Used to be a certain kind of woman—I could spot her through the revolving door. Anticipate the lush and heavy elevator ride dizzy with her Rive Gauche. The fur, well-kept but not recently won. Tenderly cared for skin, tight at the temples, going a little papery at her eyes. Not from smiling, not from a lifetime of hearty laughs. Jokes and sand tracked into the house and children knocking things over. No, that's not why her eyes look tired. Tired watching that walk by, fingers trailing over the fur, so hard-won when it was won. Tired of high heels clicking in immaculate perfection. Tired of a thousand mornings smoothing on the Oil of Olay. Renergie. Force-Vital. New from Elizabeth Arden. Or a thousand other desperate creams. Scented soft and lovely, designed to break the fall. Help break the fall. An elevator is the most intimate of spaces, I think. I can tell every product on a woman's face, body, hair in a seven-floor elevator ride. Scent, combination of scents work their way through me and I can love a woman by the twelfth floor.

I miss the Rive Gauche.

No one wears Rive Gauche anymore. It had class, a wrecked class, and sadness.

They're wearing different things now. Poison, sometimes. Chanel No. 5, of course. But it's not the same.

Sometimes I'd just sit downstairs and cry, waiting for them to buzz, order a fruit salad delivered to the room.

Something like that can—it can keep you alive for a week. Just one clear look from her eyes. A touch of her hand as she tips you. The henna-ed brass lights in her aggressively tamed hair. Just thinking of the things she might let you do. Shaving her armpits in the shower. Would she trust me? She should. I would never hurt her. Never.

My hands are very steady. A man in love is always gentle.

Something in the angle of the head and you know she used to be a dancer. And you know she's in quiet pain with every step, because she almost does see you, see *you*, when you arrive at her door bearing the fruit salad. The one she asked for. With the one grape held gently in your mouth the whole lone elevator ride up, then placed carefully back where it came from, in the position of honor at the very top.

When did it happen?

Slowly, of course, but then it was done. And did the women stop wearing Rive Gauche? Or did they just stop coming to this hotel?

Excerpt from
Valerie Shoots Andy

CARSON KREITZER

NICO is at an eternal, endless Warhol party.

NICO: I died while I was riding my bicycle. Out where the road goes next to the desert. It's very hot, very quiet. Very quiet. All you can hear is the sound of your tires crunching the little pebbles on the road.

But you wonder how I die.

(Short, odd giggle)

Me, too. It's funny.

I have a heart attack.

(Beat)

I say it's funny because it's not very interesting, is it?

How many times I should have died. Waking up, I didn't know what country I was in. My fucking beauty shot to hell. My long blue veins all shot to hell.

Twenty years, I begged Death to come and take me. In the dark, behind my eyes. But you know Death is a man. The way to get his attention

is to ignore him.

I stop. Finally, I stop.

And this is when . . . I *stop*.

I give up the needles and my heart gives up on me.

(Shrugs)

This life, you know, it doesn't let you leave. You cannot just walk away.

I was never really in the desert. I felt the heat. I felt the sweat evaporate off my body into that dry, hot air. I heard the silence all around me, silence.

But I never really left this. I was here all the time.

Kim's Arrival

KATIE LEO

The middle class home of DALE and Brenda Johnson. Dale is drinking whiskey along with his birthday cake and telling his adopted teenage daughter Kim the story of her arrival.

DALE: Oh, come on, indulge your old man in a little storytelling on his birthday! You know, as you get older, that's all you have left. Just old stories no one wants to hear anymore.

(Kim is silent. Dale drinks throughout the following.)

You came over on a plane with forty other Korean orphans. It was a huge jumbo jet full of babies, social workers, and other folks from the agency. Biggest delivery of orphans from another country we'd ever seen. The papers called it a "jet stork." I remember your mother was so nervous, she packed up this great big duffel bag full of everything you could ever think a baby would need—diapers, baby wipes, powder, toys, three changes of clothing—you name it. I mean, a baby could live off what was in that bag for months! But of course, the one thing we forgot was formula. Leave it to Brenda to forget the one essential item . . .

So, we had to stop by Perkins on the way home. We had to ask them for some milk, and they were so nice about it. That black waitress looked around the whole place and found a young couple with an extra bottle. They just gave it to us—didn't even know us! And they heated up the milk in the kitchen. Yes sir, angels were watching over us that night.

You know, when those Korean ladies came off that plane with those babies in their hands, you coulda knocked me over with a feather. I'd never seen so many dark-skinned babies, and all with full heads of hair. I mean it . . . you all had this thick, black hair! And, then they started calling off numbers and names. And your mother and I are standing there, watching everyone around us meeting their kids for the first time. And, we're thinking, "When's it gonna be our turn? What if there was a mistake?" But, finally we heard our number called and our name. We walked up to those ladies and the one lady standing there with you in her arms, and it was like God himself had hand-picked you from the streets of Korea and carried you to us . . .

It was like all those months of trying to get pregnant, all the tests, the questions, the pressure, everyone asking, "When? When?"—all that pain was just meant to happen. And, that mean old social worker, Mrs. Lathrop, who discouraged us from adopting you because she didn't believe in white people raising an Oriental—even suffering through that bitch's endless questions was worth it. Your mother's right. You were perfect, Kim. Our perfect little girl.

(Dale reaches his hand out to his daughter. She recoils and stands quickly. There is a moment of awkward silence that is broken by the sound of a car horn from outside. Kim grabs her purse from behind the couch.)

Excerpt from
American Sublime

PATRICIA LYNCH

TODD: Have you ever heard of a messenger? No, no, don't look at me like that. I am not I repeat talking in circles. It's just that—did you ever see any of those movies where the kid and the dad are in a crowded subway or train station and they're out for a good time together, baseball game—whatever, and they run into some bum who mutters something innocuous and strange, now that's your arch-typical messenger—but the dad blows by intent on the game—and when the train comes and the doors open and people start flooding out and in, somehow the dad loses the son. He loses his son. And usually in these movies there's some other danger as if freakin' subway stations aren't dangerous enough, there's a killer or killers who are look-ing for the kid or some such thing. So just going home is not really an option. Anyway the man goes berserk trying to pry the doors open to get to his son, and tries running after the train and then going to the next station . . . You've seen these movies right—and then he goes to the cops and they all start looking all over and no one can find his son. He's disappeared, gone. It's his fate. The wife is crying and blaming the man as if it was solely his fault—well, you sit there in the dark and you swear you will never let that happen to you. NOT GOING TO HAPPEN. And what do you do, you come up with a plan, a fool-proof simple plan—YOU FIX THINGS, YOU'RE A MAN. So what is that plan you ask, what is that plan? Alli Alli All in Free!

(Beat)
Alli Alli All in Free!

See, I've got to believe that there's a place like that. A Home Free. A neutral spot, in a safe place that you can go, the kid can go, anyone in the know can go, no matter what shit is coming down, no matter what has befallen you, get there and you're home free. Because you go there, you wait there—eventually you will hook up with your loved one and escape fate.

(Beat)
And so this is that. And that's why I'm here.

Excerpt from *Mad Love*

JENNIFER MAISEL

TED mourns the loss of the life he was supposed to have.

TED: This is not the life I was supposed to have. You only get one chance at this stuff. Everything's going along as planned. You work to fulfill expectations. And there it is, lying out in front of you like the next stretch of highway you're about to cover. Road signs. Motel 6s. Detours. They're all supposed to lead you to the same destination.

Adam—He was the first thing I did right in the world. According to plan. I was afraid to touch him when he was born. Afraid I might slip up and he'd be lost, so quickly. I would have liked to think it was an accident. I would have liked to think I was one of those fathers he could have confided in. I would have liked to think that I would have seen the warning signs, that his life was tinged with happiness and hope. Remember Dad, he said the night before he did it, remember the hill of death? Remembering that moment when he wasn't sure his bike would make it down the hill unscathed . . . It's a lot smaller now, he said. It doesn't give that rush of life anymore, he said. He didn't understand we outgrow that.

I heard her scream and I found them. I couldn't stop thinking that the last time I saw his body that mottled blue color was the day he was born.

I would have liked to hope that he'd never know the black days of being alive.

Nobody gives a shit about how I feel.

There must be a way to do these things right.

This was not the way my life was supposed to happen.

Not Everybody Has a General Lee from *Hazard County*

ALLISON MOORE

CHAD, a seventeen-year-old high school student, white. He is middle class, maybe upper middle class. Wears slightly urban clothes, and maybe a ball cap. An expensive-looking watch. Speaks with a slight drawl, but nothing comic. He occasionally uses rap or hip-hop gestures.

CHAD: People think it's cool, I guess. I mean, it's—you know, I'm out, and people know it's me, they know right away 'Chad's pulling up,' whatever, because, you know, not everybody has a *General Lee.* So it causes a stir, a little bit of a stir. I like that.
(Very exaggerated and slightly aggressive)
"The Chicks Dig It."
(Laughs)
Naw. I mean,
(As before)
I mean THEY DO.
(Pause, then smile)
I've been working on it for about four years. My dad used to race stockcars? He was an amateur and all, 'cause, you know he actually had a business to run, he's not some loser. But he's always working on something. And we were out one day because he wanted to look at this '68 Cutlass Supreme? So we go around back a this guy's house to check out his setup, and there it is, '69 Charger up on blocks. Total POS, engine completely out, but I flipped, because it's the exact right year. I was only like, thirteen, but my dad bought it for me for eight hundred bucks, which sounds like a lot, but. There's a lot of collectors. My dad helped

99

me rebuild the engine, struts, all that. And the specs for the paint job are all online.

Some a my friends tried to make fun of me at first, 'cause I was like building a car I couldn't even drive? But now they're like "Dawg, that car is *rip*," and "Lemme drive it, catch some air, do it Duke-style," all that. My buddy Clay even got the Luke Duke Slide down, you know, where he slides across the hood and then jumps in the car?

We were out one time, on our way up to Clay's cabin, and we stop at this gas station. And this guy, total fucking hick, he sees the car and he starts in, just "Yeeeeee-haw!" All the way across the parking lot, just "Yee-haw!" like they did in the show. And Clay's all "Check this cracker," and the guy starts heading right for us, which I'm pretty used to now, and most folks are nice. But he's just this—got the gap teeth, and scraggly-ass hair, fucking reeks of, like, piss and Colt 45, and he's all "Lookie here! It's Bo and Luke! All the way from Hazzard County!" And we talk for minute, and finally I'm like, I gotta go, nice to know ya. And I unlock the door and he flips. "You ain't even welded the doors shut! You can't have a General Lee with doors that open! Boy, you got to slide through the window." And Clay looks at the guy and says, real serious: "I know it never rained in Hazzard, sir, but it sure does come down sometimes in Cony-ers." And the guy looks confused, he's like, "What?" And Clay says, "Well, Bo and Luke could keep their windows down all the time, but my friend here sure doesn't want his interior to get wet when it rains." And the guy, just total classic, looks at Clay and says, "Son, were you dropped on your head? When it rains, you just put the windows up, dumb ass!"

(*Chad laughs.*)

It's Subversive from
Hazard County

ALLISON MOORE

MARTIN, thirties, white. Wears stylish clothes. Ivy League academic.

MARTIN: It's brilliant, in a way, *The Dukes of Hazzard* is actually brilliant, which is why I have my students study it. You know, people try to dismiss it—this university tried to "dismiss it" from my syllabus, in fact—by saying that the show is nothing more than a collection of cliché and stereotype. But they *play* with the clichés, they *play* with the stereotypes. Particularly in the first two seasons. It can easily be argued—and what I, in fact, argue—is that what they are actually doing is *high camp.* Which is always a subversive act.

Now, now, there is, in discussing this, always some debate about whether or not this was intentional on the part of the creators of the show. And I argue vehemently in the affirmative. As example: they place the character of Daisy Duke in short shorts, with pantyhose and *stilettos,* and send her to the chicken coop to collect eggs.

That's subversive.

You see what I'm saying? If they would have had her in bare feet, and no stockings, but still the short shorts, that would have been *merely* stereotypical, and, and consequently, exploitative and catering to the lowest common denominator. But what they do instead is take our collective fantasy of what life is like on a simple country farm, and, through exaggeration, literally throw it back in our faces.

I liken it to the contemporary incarnation of the *wife beater.* You know, the way the term *wife beater* has come to denote the tight, ribbed, white tank top of, of, the Mafia-era Dago, or the current backwoods trailer trash. And young men and adolescents and, and, lesbians, in a very conscious and ironic way have co-opted the wife beater. The wearer consciously evokes our collective cultural image of an *actual,* ah, spouse abuser. He wants you to look at him and simultaneously see the potential for real violence, and that that potential is a *joke.*

If it was *only* a joke, then it would be a costume. It would have no power.

It's the same thing, the entire use of the "Good ol' boy" stereotype.

That's the brilliance of the *Dukes of Hazzard.* It's both the joke, and the danger behind the joke.

The Reverend Graham Explains His Cracker

KIRA OBOLENSKY

THE REVEREND SYLVESTER GRAHAM addresses the audience. He is stern, and vaguely hysterical. Quite thin, and hungry.

Let me ask each and every one of you sinners a question.

What did you have for dinner tonight?

A piece of prime rib? Dressed, perhaps, in a sauce made from red wine and butter? Accompanied by a puree of potatoes, white and frothy with New Hampshire cream?

Or perhaps, you have determined that red meat in a pool of its own blood is too rich and have decided upon the breast of a chicken. Plump, no doubt, dolloped with a mustard reduction, served with peas, lost forever in a buttery pond.

You opted, perchance, for a thick oxtail soup, under the presumption that a soup will be lighter fare, even if composed of mortal bones.

I am about to discuss dessert, for one look at you all gathered here gives me certainty that you have indulged. I can see it on your faces. The smug comfort that sweetness lends.

(He composes himself.)

It is in this part of the meal that all hope of salvation goes south. The current fashion for chocolate melted and whipped, silken to the tongue, laced with liqueur, reduces all mortals into a quivering mass of pleasure.

Who amongst us doesn't salivate?

I do not.

I cannot. For I am alarmed!

The richness of our food is corrupting our very soul! It is undermining our very natures! It is giving us a host of ailments that I will elucidate later in my lecture that contribute to a grand sickness! Our diet leads us, most certainly, into a future where we are ruled by appetite, crazed with desires, overweight, and oversexed.

We have become a nation in search of the next delectable morsel. Ruled by pleasure, what will happen to us if we eat whatever we desire? Will we become so soft and spineless as to renounce the very freedoms that make us?

It is difficult to separate sin from nourishment, for of course, the food that makes us ill, also nourishes us. Let me make an analogy to the paintings you might see on display in a so-called museum of culture. Why, if you were to look at a painting of a landscape perhaps perfect in its balance of green and ochre—and then the colors were to shift ever so slightly to become delicious—why the artist has lied for our pleasure—the painter has ruined our eyes—the same way chefs ruin our tongues—he has made us want more beauty from a world that cannot deliver.

I am, let us be perfectly clear, speaking about lust. About an overload of the senses. About the connection, proven again and again, between appetites. The desire to consume, whether it be meat or woman, overheats us sexually and is directly related to a string of dire maladies.

A curve in the spine? It is surely connected to what appears on the young boy's plate. Later, at night, perhaps he writhes under his covers, too comfortable in his privacy. Pulmonary consumption. A voluptuous woman, her beauty exaggerated, too ripe with flesh, who eats whatever she desires. Voluptuous—why even this word is too much to say! And who enjoys her voluptuousness, but the man next door, who I dare say sometimes joins her for both dinner and sin. Such a woman is sure to find herself at the doctor's office in a matter of time, coughing up blood.

Hysteria. An ailment that seems to afflict everyone in society today, be they man or woman. Witness the female of the species with her high-pitched wheeze and moan—in bed for weeks at a time, massaging the temples, cursing their loved ones, screaming to expel the foul wind in their bowels.

And men, impatient with their bankers, enraged at basic social exchanges, whipped into a foul fury by a stray dog? By a stubborn horse? By the state of our union?

The cause of such hysteria, and this has been scientifically proven by anecdotes that come to us from Boston, is the ketchup and mustard we so liberally apply to our repasts. Bostonians, it must be said, eat more of the aforementioned spreads than others, and it is primarily in Boston where we see such cases of hysteria as to make even the governor concerned.

I must end my list with the ailment that afflicts so many Americans that it could be epidemic! Constipation. Confess my friend! Who among you have added to the sins of dinner by consuming a dinner roll? Oh, the evils inherent in refined flour. The audacity of millers to remove everything natural from wheat. The dinner roll. So very easy to eat, why one barely needs to chew. Is that why we must eat so much of it? While much of my comments on white flour can be found in my Treatise against Bakers, suffice it to say that constipation rests primary among our ailments caused by diet.

And so, I present to you all today a way out of this nefarious web of carnal urges. A way to stop the ailments that plague our health. A method by which we can purge both body and soul. An end to constipation, which surely is brought on by God to make a point each time we must wrestle with our bowels.

My outline for complete reform can be found in a brochure offered by the chaste lady outside our meeting hall. In this brochure, you will see a rendering of a landscape in black ink, so as not to assume any freedoms, the bare outline of a house, wooden and simple, a sketch of a camp where one can come to reclaim their sanity and their consumption of food. A week in my camp will bring you back to the proper notion of what food should be. It will remove all desires from your bodies; a week of my regime and you are cured. If you are interested, please sign your name on the lady's book.

In the meantime, here is what I suggest:

Renounce meat! All meat, even if it is soup! Avoid the lamb, for it is truly a wolf! Leave cows to graze in their pastures. The chicken's breast deserves to avoid your plates! Embrace vegetables. Avoid too much butter. Drink only water. No matter the weather, sleep with your windows open. Be cheerful when you eat.

And supplement your diet with this modest cracker.

(He holds up a graham cracker.)

An invention of mine I call the Graham cracker. I have named it after myself, lest anyone think the cracker is meant to be a culinary treat. This cracker, not a cake, is a simple food, made from Graham flour, also named for myself—a meal ground from wheat and cooked with water and a few spices. A cracker destined to become known for its powers of salvation. My Graham cracker has been cooked to soak up indulgences of appetite. It is a cracker, I believe, destined to stop the course this country has set so irrevocably.

Listen to its dry snap.

(He breaks it.)

There is no pleasure in such a sound.

The texture is as honest as homespun wool.

The flavor—

Unadulterated.

(He eats.)

Eat one and be saved.

Excerpt from *Saturn*

DOMINIC ORLANDO

FATHER as a young man appears. A ghost, a memory.

FATHER: Carpentry takes patience. Edges need sanding—lines have to match up—it's what I imagine praying must be like.
(Beat)
It's hard to be a carpenter when you lack patience. When you have to sneak your breaths. My son Paul calls it Terror. Terror of what? Failing to match up the lines? Failing in life? Or failure of each single breath? What did I teach my children? Can a family be cursed? You used to hear about curses all the time. *La malocchio.* The evil eye.
(Laugh)
Some ancestor makes a choice—and generations suffer for it. The words are different now—it's all science. I used to read science. Velikosky. Ages of Chaos. Worlds in Collision. Science. Chemicals in the brain. Neurotransmitters. Schizophrenia. "Split mind." But can a family be cursed?
(Beat)
I was the youngest of five. My parents were both born in Italy, my mother and my father—I think of myself as an American. I always have. We had a big house on Long Island when I was a boy. I was very young, but in my memory it seems like a big house, a big—life. On Long Island. Then my father died—very suddenly—
(He snaps his fingers.)
—and the house was gone. Everything—changed. I was just a boy. We moved to a small apartment in Brooklyn. My mother sat me down on her lap in a white wooden chair and turned on the stove. The room filled up with gas. She closed the windows and the doors—everything was shut up tight. The room filled

up with gas. I sat on her lap. Her mouth was a thin line. I touched the mole above her lip. The room filled up with gas. My brother came home in a wordless panic—I think he was fifteen. He threw open the windows and the doors and I'm not sure but I think I never took another breath as long as I lived. Can a family be cursed? An ancestor makes a choice, and generations suffer . . .

I wanted to be a pilot when the war came, but I had some trouble breathing and they wouldn't let me fly—Hitler was defeated, and so was I . . . when I came home, I went to UCLA on the GI Bill—I saw myself as an executive, or a—I saw myself . . . I dropped out midway through my freshman year . . . my life began to lose shape . . .

Worlds in Collision. Ages of Chaos. Chaos. "A condition of total disorder or confusion." I used to read the dictionary—no kidding. I used to sit in my chair in the living room of the shabby little house we would've never afforded without my wife's mother—I used to sit in my chair flipping through the dictionary. There's nothing liberating about chaos—nothing artistic, or brave. The Greek means "empty space." Empty. And still people have the most romantic ideas about chaos, insanity—Split Mind. I think these people must have led very safe lives, they must be so safe and secure it makes them sick. Because if they really knew anything about chaos—about total disorder in an empty space—if the air became water when they tried to breathe—if science didn't *work*—they would, they would—

(Mozart's Gran Partita *plays softly, building.*)

They would listen to Mozart. They might be afraid to move. Afraid to breathe. Afraid to touch their wife. Afraid to love their children. But even in that empty space they could listen.

(He conducts gently.)

And as they listened they might see a piece of something so delicate and precious, so mysterious, it would almost be like breathing, it would almost be like rising out of that chair, out of that empty space, rising up and embracing something even pilots never see—and they would wish, not for chaos, but for sanity, for one clean breath of air—the sanity of Mozart, the sanity of da Vinci. Of Cole Porter. Duke Ellington. HOW CAN YOU SAY THE ONLY THING I EVER GAVE YOU WAS TERROR?!? I see you listen to my music. I see the Raymond Chandler beside Paul's bed. The old movies. And you all play tennis. Except for Paul, who was too afraid of me to let me teach him. But Marco and Thomas play. Donny is a pro. I taught you that. And we sat, the four of us, on weekends, we sat in that horrible little room and watched the games. And I tried to make you see what I saw, I tried to tell you. But I could never crack open the thin line of my mouth.

(He mimes the tennis moves.)

The forehand. The backhand. The lob. The ace! The rush to the net. The silent grace of their movements, the delicacy of their skill, the beauty of their strength. The. Elegance. That's what I gave you, Paul—your love of elegance.

(Something strikes him.)

Elegance *and* Terror—Split Mind.

(He snaps his fingers and the light on him goes black.)

Excerpt from
Do You Know a Secret?

DANIEL PINKERTON

This play takes place in Berlin between 1988 and 1993 (before and after the fall of the Berlin Wall). The action alternates between live scenes and filmed monologues; the filmed monologues in Act I take place years earlier. This monologue is the opening of the play, filmed eighteen years before the first scene.

WALTER: I first met Karin six months ago, at the parade that opened the Twenty-First Annual Week of German-Soviet Friendship. Who could forget such an event? The tall, bear-like Comrade Brezhnev himself, leader of our "friends," bent down to kiss Secretary Ulbricht, a hundred pigeons were released, and billions of *Ostmarks'* worth of Russian-built tanks, fresh from the invasion of Prague—excuse me, the "August Assistance"—began rolling down *Unter den Linden*, followed by row after row of soldiers in perfect formation, their bayonets gleaming in the morning sun. The sight of so much "security" was a stirring visual metaphor for our German Democratic Republic.

Well, undoubtedly you were there, too. It was *dienstlich*—our duty. And in the middle of all this goodwill and celebration of everything that keeps us safe from capitalism, I saw . . . Karin. Blonde hair, little woolly cap, marching at the head of a ragged band of perhaps twenty foolish citizens. I've no idea who they were. I didn't *want* to know who they were. But there was something very . . . arresting—*(Smiles)* sorry!—about Karin. For one thing, she carried an enormous sign proclaiming END STASI TORTURE.

How should I know? I proof the party paper, but I don't really follow politics. Still, a sign like that makes you wonder:

Do the police *really* torture people? And then—as I'm sure you know—the Stasi fired rubber bullets and tear gas into the crowd. Now I make no judgments. But people panicked and began to flee, and what did the Stasi do? They moved in with gas and truncheons, spoiling the mood of "peace through strength" that the parade had engendered. I daresay Comrade Brezhnev was not pleased.

I myself did not flee. I found myself moving *toward* Karin, which is quite unlike me. But I wanted to become involved . . . In the clash? No. With Karin. I was attracted to her. So I pushed my way through the crowd. My eyes were smarting from the gas, but I managed to keep sight of Karin's sign. And just as I reached her, a policeman swung a club at her, and she fell to the street and dropped it.

This was my chance. I could have lifted up Karin. I could have picked up the sign. But I was frozen—suspended between desire and fear. She looked, at that moment, quite helpless. And yet I knew she was strong, possibly intoxicating, and certainly dangerous. As the police dragged us both away, I knew that I had failed some sort of test, that I was too . . . *careful* to ever be a part of Karin Niedermann's world.

Excerpt from *Three Seasons*

MARK ROSENWINKEL

FRANKLIN is the former President of the United States. Once a vibrant and vigorous figure, he has recently undergone some kind of a spiritual and physical transformation. He now goes about in a wheelchair and speaks to a young White House aide on the patio of a secret mountain retreat in New England.

FRANKLIN: This world is a lie, son. Why do you expect anything different? Give me your hand. I used to sit out here, in this very spot. Only a few minutes at a time. For a few minutes, I'd be transported. And . . . I know this all sounds strange, son, but believe me, it's the truth . . . What I didn't know then was that this, out here, was a window. A tiny window into a world of grace and sanity, and gentility. Truman knew it. Hell, they all did. A window to something real and full-blooded and . . . how can I say it? Connected. Five minutes at a time. And then I always had to shut it out, and return to the madness and the confusion. It was too frightening, Thomas. The thought, the prospect that I could actually cut myself free. That I could drift on the wind, one moment to the next. Oh, yes, that was frightening. So we pull back, every time. But now, I don't pull back. No, now I can sit here and wait for the wind, like I'm some exotic Oriental kite, with streamers and wings. Wait for the wind to catch me up, and fly . . .

(He closes his eyes and sways in the wind.)

Close your eyes. Pray. To whatever God, whatever force of man or nature which transcends this world of uncertainty. Pray. Pray for all of us. Pray for wings.

Excerpt from *Sirius Rising*

GWENDOLYN SCHWINKE

The CHORUS *is the spirit of Oren, a middle-aged farmer who has been murdered by his brother. Here he tells his own story.*

CHORUS (OREN): He feels the farm slipping out of his hands, trickling away like dirt through his fingers. His mother's farm, his father's farm, and on back in the family. The fields where they worked, the woods where they hunted, the river and ponds full of fish. He visits those places, wanders the farm and thinks how it seemed he farmed with his Daddy long after his Daddy had passed away.

He thinks, "If only I had managed better." He takes all the blame, but shouldering the blame won't save the farm. He says to himself,

"Sometimes I wish I was a kid again And my Daddy still alive.
When I did something wrong
If I would just 'fess up
And accept blame for what I did
Then he'd help me make it right."

Always a way to fix things. Like the time he dented the car by backing into the hay wagon. Didn't help the wagon much, either. They got it fixed, and he worked off the cost of it. In desperation now, he says to his Daddy:

"I'm sorry, I messed up.
I'm doing a bad job, here in this drought
Looks like I'm going to lose the farm
My fault, Dad, and I'll admit it.
Please, tell me what to do."

And his Daddy does answer back
(I can't say as I believe in ghosts

Or people communicating from beyond the grave
But you live with somebody or something so long
It's like they're in you
One and the same
You, your parents, and the land.)
The answer he gets back from his Daddy:
"Oren, I don't see
No way to fix it."

Excerpt from
Thrown by Angels

GWENDOLYN SCHWINKE

MARKO, a television producer, tells his friend Toni about a love affair he had when he was in seminary.

MARKO: Well. Love and passion aren't synonyms—you forget that. You know how it goes, you fall hard for somebody and it just knocks that sort of useful information right out of your head. You know what I mean? You meet someone who's passionate about something, like . . . he stays up all night playing the saxophone . . .

You fall in love because you see the passion in this person, and you imagine that when he turns his gaze on you, naturally the passion will shine out from his eyes in your direction. And then you find out. Those shining rays are focused on the mountains, the saxophone . . . or something like, say . . . moving up in the hierarchy of a very traditional church. And if you spend any time in this person's gaze, well, you're naturally in between him and the object of his passion, aren't you? You're an obstacle. Two things can happen with obstacles—they can be avoided. Or they can be destroyed.

Excerpt from *Burning Jenny*

BUFFY SEDLACHEK

GILL MAN: One-fifth of that air going into your lungs, that air all around you, movin' in and out of you is oxygen—it can blow you right up! All it takes is speed. You could breathe too fast, go outa control, and then you got trouble.

Air's just waitin' for you to get up enough speed, so it can move through you fast enough for oxygenation. Air—up your nose, down your throat, in your lungs, and—BAM!—ignition!

OXYGENATION! All the parts of you combinin' with oxygen fast enough to make fire! It's just a matter of time. Breathe too fast just once, just one time, and BOY! You got fire in your lungs, up your tubes, out your mouth, out your nose, across the floor, up the wall, out the window, off the porch, down the block, and up the highway and blow your world apart.

Cleansing conflagration is waitin' to start right inside you.

How can you sleep? Don't sleep! Wake up!!! Wake up!! Wake Up!!!

(Pause)

You should learn to breathe water.

Excerpt from *Circus Buff*

BUFFY SEDLACHEK

GILBERT is a circus trainer.

GILBERT: Hell, yes, we can put you up on a trapeze. But, don't expect to go anywhere, don't expect to FLY. You can expect to Fall, into the net. Lemme tell ya about the aerodynamics of leapin'. The leaper being the one flyin' into the arms of the catcher.

Well, the perfect leapin' body would be—a boy. A BOY— with strong shoulders. You got breasts they just get in the way. You got hips—you might as well go home. BUT—if you're a girl and you wanna leap—you better be SHORT. Five-foot-three or shorter. Good strong shoulders for the size of 'em and flat, flat chest, fine, fine boned. Little bird-bones. Now, the bird-bones can carry a LITTLE hip, I said a LITTLE. And, NO body fat. Not. One. Ounce.

I can count the girl leapers on less than two hands and the good ones I can count on a mitten. BOYS—they'll be the ones to pump and get that great lift in the backswing that launches 'em sweet to the catcher.

'Course, if they birth a baby, the hips widen out—and there goes the act. 'Course, they'll try the breast removal surgery—but that just weakens the muscle wall.

Knew a leaper-girl—she got this doctor to shave her hip bones. A few centimeters on each side . . . gave her the aerodynamics she needed—but, 'course she come up pregnant and that was a waste.

'Course, another girl, she got herself a hysterectomy—took the eggs and all, and them artificial hormones kept her nice and narrow in the hip—and the hormones gave her breast cancer and she got 'em cut off, and—Dang she was a good leaper—almost a BOY—almost.

So, you go on now, cut off your breasts, cut out your womb, shave your hip bones, and while you're at it, your head, amputation at the knee, the ankle or the hip, lose your feet—and you can be a leaper. And after you cut it all off, and you're standin' there, as androgynous as you can get—you will still be a GIRL, and around here the REAL boys will fly first.

My Brother, Sandro

ROSANNA STAFFA

I make games for myself. I walk in the Armani store, Fiorucci, Bruno Magli and try things on for my brother. I say to myself: Sandro would like this. That's the name I gave him, Sandro. Why? Sandro. I don't know. Well whatever. It's fine. I can't tell you anything I don't know. I try on all sorts of things. It can make you seasick, the tiny fitting room, the mirrors. You can see your profile. Your butt even. I can't believe how picky Sandro is. Linen shirts, silk ties, little black nothings I can squeeze in my fist. My, is he picky. Sandro can send me back for the right thing twenty times. That doesn't leave me much time for myself. No time. I can't believe it at the end of the day. Wouldn't that be nice, to do something for myself one time. Take the subway and go to the end of the Green Line, where the subway comes up, and you see the sky. My cigarettes, a CD player. Can you imagine going 'till the train stops? That's where they find all the umbrellas left under the seats. And then me, sitting there. Well, I should clean up the house first, but letting go of the house gives you freedom. I read it in a magazine. They were real serious about it, three pages straight, no pictures. I couldn't believe it. There are cups, forks, knives in my sink. Newspapers and special offer fliers on the table, on the floor. My socks have a hole, I have no time. Before going to bed, at night I kneel on the carpet, crouch over the classified. It's good for my sleep. It's so good you should try it. A leading truck company, airport area, has immediate need of a sharp, experienced accountant, non-smoker. So does Martini, Rossi, Betton and Bisson. PO Box 3844 seeks an artist full or part time for hand painting on ceramics. It's so tender! Really. I know what you're saying, it's a mess. But look. It's 1982 in these newspapers. March 18. You can see it, right? The sharp, experienced accountant, leading blue trucks farther and farther into the very core of the country, carrying easy-to-assemble cockpits and wings. They arrived. They all arrived. See what I mean? There are pages and pages of ads, urgently seeking, generously compensating, immediately hiring. They are all happy now! Pages and pages! Siena Advertising, Capra Bros., H & A Architects. Happy! Happy! You're lazy, my father says. The distance of the memory makes his voice muffled. Like it comes from under the sink. You're so lazy, he says. You'll end up alone with forty cats. He says, remember not to light a cigarette to three different people with the same match. Remember. The younger one dies. Sure. I was a kid what do I know? That's when Sandro and I started smoking. I mean, in my dreams. Sandro and I were teensy then. I made him up in my head same age as me. He loved everything I loved. Everything! We played together all day. Sandro do this, Sandro come here. I lit cigarette after cigarette in my dreams. One for me, one for my father, one for my mother. Cigarette after cigarette, like a prayer. My mother in the dreams had all her hair back from chemo, lipstick on her lips. I lit cigarette after cigarette in my dreams, one match for three. When my mother died, Sandro didn't want to come to the hospital to see her dead. No and no! He refused. He banged his head and fists against the wall. Like this! My father and I had to wait and wait by the car. In the snow. What do you know? Sandro curled up in the big closet in my mother's bedroom and didn't want to come. Didn't want to come out. No and no! The more you know about Sandro, the less you know. He doesn't want to come out. See? He hugs his knees among my mother's old shoes, the camel hair robe, the blue and gray skirts. I try and lure him out. This, that. I'd swear he'd like a silk shirt with the initials of Calvin Klein on the pocket. You would, right? Do you think he does? I go back to the stores. I exchange the clothes for Sandro many times. The salespeople know me now. They sigh. Raise their eyes to the ceiling when I walk in again. And again. The sales slip is ready in my hand. I explain. Sandro does not have a job, he does not have a girlfriend, he does not have a friend. He has nobody, I explain.

Waltz

ROSANNA STAFFA

It's a clear night. I dance from wall to wall: Tango. I am Spanish tonight, see? See my back? Arched in dark desires. Women applaud, in the dark. The sound of their hands, hear it? Look at my cot, a bed sheet entangled in a twisted scrawl, shiny from my sweat, like entrails. In ancient Rome, priests slept under the stars, visited by ghosts. Learnt from the entrails of sheep whose army would win, whose throat would be slashed, whose fingers, eyes. This is my face. The right side is raw. I touch, here and there, tap, feel around. Mouth, nose, eyebrows. Like a child exploring a doll. My right side responds with pain, electric. I go back. Tap, feel. This is my face. They tied my hands behind my back, put a blindfold over my eyes, said, "Listen carefully." In the silence there was my voice, screaming, as in a dream, in the night. I still said, this is my voice. It's mine. "Hear that?" they asked. A jackal, a vulture. This is my voice, I said. In Spain I have small dancing feet, I dance moving my waist side to side and around. A small tugging at the ribs. I'm on my knees on the concrete floor. Shuffle wall to wall, humming. I wrapped my ankles in the dishrag and a shirt, I am the male little mermaid. The one and only. My legs are broken. They said, "Listen to this." There was no sound of tearing, cracking, just my voice. My voice calling, calling. Tentative, at first. It was a name I didn't recognize. This I remember: her voice. She said, Follow. She said, Here, follow me. She was whispering. She said, Shift your weight on the left foot, like this. The floor tiles were cracked, brown. My soles left a damp trail, like the one my index finger, wet with saliva, used to trace on windowpanes as a child. Secret messages to God, unreadable to the human eye. She said, This is a waltz. Her feet folded like scissor blades across the tiles. I sleep sitting on the floor, my back against the wall. I fall on my side at each dream. I wake up. Start again. I had a dream, I say to them while they pull my head up and back, it was a true dream. I see the reflection of my face in the tub of water at my feet. They want me to float like a fish, seeking air, air. They hold my head down in the water, I am a goldfish blowing bubbles, dying. I am a child in a long summer afternoon, tapping my fingers on the windowpanes. Opening and closing my mouth. Dying. They want names, names and addresses. Dates when I did this, that. And that. They walk me down a dark hallway. Out in the courtyard. I fall. Get up. Again. They hold me up. I fall again. My shadow falls. I watch my shadow fall and curl up on the dirt. I cannot walk, I say. They try to lock my shadow to their shadows, upright. I cannot walk, I say. She said, Dance with me. Will you? I said, I cannot dance. She said, Yes, yes. Just follow me. She said, Dance with me. Will you? I said, I cannot dance. She said, Yes, yes. Just follow me. She touched my cheek lightly, with her fingertips. Remember me, she said. I remember you. I remember.

Untitled

ALLAN STAPLES

JIMMY, dressed in a suit and tie, speaks to the audience.

JIMMY *(brightly):* Don't I look snazzy? Pretty nice, huh? It's for my funeral. Oh no, don't feel bad for me; I'm much better off now. Anyways, I'm here because this is your lucky day because, before I go, I get to offer you a little insight, a little insider info if you will as to what the sweet hereafter brings. That's right, I'm gonna answer the big questions for you right now. Ready? When you die, there is actually a bright white light. But when it happens, you don't know if it's heaven or if it's your body shutting down. And, honestly, you don't care 'cause what would it matter anyway? And two, there is an afterlife. And let me tell you, heaven lives up to the fucking hype. I'll tell you that much. I mean, it's not paradise per se, but it's still not a bad way to spend eternity. I mean, think Jimi Hendrix opening for Frank Sinatra every single night. That's what it is. Of course your relatives are all there, and your pets are there, too. The dead ones, at least. It turns out Pet Heaven and People Heaven are close to each other so that's a good deal. But, like all great deals there is a catch. Strings, of course, have got to be attached. With all of this wonderfulness, with all of this quiet, there comes this . . . tiny bit of knowledge. This nugget of wisdom. The Solution to a mystery you never knew you were living. Life's last cruel ironic twist. You wanna know what mine was? I was a naturally gifted piano player. Yeah that's right. All those years, all the time wasted playing the stupid guitar and the equally stupid lessons. And I woulda been a really really good piano player if only I had tried. I always kinda liked the piano, too, we even had one here. But, you know, we'd use it for a coffee table, for eating off of, you know, for virtually every other use than a piano. God, the piano. Yeah, it's pretty much the thing that would kill ya if you weren't already dead. I didn't know. But you never can know until it's too late.

Excerpt from *Magnificent Waste*

CARIDAD SVICH

The YOUNG MAN appears. He wears a feather boa and sequins on his nipples.

YOUNG MAN: I got dressed up. I wanted to go to a party. I needed a place to crash. I took this boa from my friend Cindy. She has lots of boas. She doesn't mind sharing them. She's great about that. She dolled me up. She says I could be on TV. "You just need a lot of sequins, baby."

I don't mind. I like shiny things: shiny houses, shiny furniture, people that gleam. I've always liked that. And candy, sure. It keeps you going. It's sugar. Sugar is the purest high. I get stoked on jellybeans. I'm on a constant rush. I walk in with my boa. Everybody notices me. I'm like the Silver Surfer. You remember him? He was a comic-book hero. I like comic books. They're like real life. Except for the fantasy shit. But the other parts feel real, y'know? I like being looked at. I don't have to say anything and people come to me. I'm like a fucking star. Electric wired. Everybody wants to touch me. They want to steal my beauty. I can tell. I let them for a while. I like playing games. When I was a kid, I played with marbles. Cool surfaces, clear glass marbles. I won every time. There are all sorts of people at this party. They have high-toned voices but inside they're rough. I can tell. I can see straight through them. It's a weird scene. I like it. I like being weird. I like being fucking out of myself. I could do anything here. I could drink anything, smoke anything, fuck anything. It's like fucking heaven. And I can crash. I can sleep on a rug, in a corner. I can slip away to another room and nobody will notice. 'Cause everybody's into something. Into a conversation or something they're looking at or . . . I can have people look at me, want me, do with me or I cannot. It's a kind of power I have. I know this. I'm good at this. I'm a doll. That's the word I hear the most. "Doll." I think it's funny. 'Cause I'm not Barbie. I mean, I've got good legs and slim hips, but that's about it. If you want breasts, you got to look at somebody else. But people say "doll" anyway. And I flash my teeth. I stick out my tongue. I act shy and then I put my fist in. It's a game. It's all a game. I just need a place to crash, sleep over, get shut-eye. I haven't slept in weeks. People want to give me things: little puffy things with meat on a plate, oily things in a bowl . . . The food here is small. It comes at you in waves. You have to be quick or you'll miss it. There's a woman in the corner painting someone's face with a marker. She looks at me. She's got anger written all over her. That's her game. I can tell. She comes up to me. She starts to paint me. She writes words on my chest and stomach and arms and legs. She's writing words all over me. "Signatures," she says. That's what she calls them. She's getting into it. She's putting on a show for the rest of the people at the party. She pulls at my boa. She wants to dance with me. I feel like I'm at Bungalow 8. There's a techno-tango mix in the background. I've got words all over my body written in this black marker, and this woman is grabbing at me. She's moving. She's letting her anger out through this song that's playing. And she's got me. We start to mimic each other. Our bodies start to speak a choral language. This is not about sex, but about moving, sheer movement. My sequins dazzle; I flip my boa. She turns. She spies me. We dare each other. The game has revved up. I can't feel anything. Everything's too loud, and all the weird pockets in this scene crowd each other. I just want to crash. I just want to sleep. I just want some-body to hold me. I'm sick of sex. I'm sick of love. I'm sick of everything. I want to be the Silver Surfer. I want to ride, and stay in my comic-book dream. I want to rub off all these words she's painted on me and give them back to somebody, put them back in the dictionary. I want to stop drinking and putting things in my mouth. I want to stop eating. Take off my sequins, take off my boa. Look at me.

The Retreating World

NAOMI WALLACE

An Iraqi man, in his late twenties, enters. He is dressed casually, in slacks and a T-shirt. He is balancing a book on his head.

Nowadays you can pick up a book like this for next to nothing. Whole libraries, years and years of careful selection and loving looks, and maybe some reading, set out by the side of the road. For sale. For next to nothing. Unfortunately I bought this one before. Before. And it cost me. But it was worth it.

(He tilts his head and lets the book drop on the stage.)

Books can be used for many things besides reading.

(He gives the book a couple of short, quick kicks.)

For exercising the ankles and toes with short, controlled bursts of movement. Or

(He snatches up the book.)

a book can be used to create a man with a bookish face. It can be done.

(He holds the book to hide his face for a moment.)

I never had the knack for telling good jokes. The kind that slap your face and send your head spinning. My friend Samir Saboura, he could tell jokes. Once he told me a joke about rice pudding, two porcupines, and a jockstrap; I laughed so hard I broke a tooth.

But this, this is a book on bird "fancying" as they say in the north of England. It took me ages to understand even though I am fluent in English and have read Macaulay's speeches in order to really hear the English language. But this was not English. This was north of English and about pigeons and doves. Not stuff for the faint hearted.

It is a deadly serious book. One suspects, after fifty pages or so, that in fact it is not a book about keeping birds as a hobby, but something far more . . . important. Like how to keep your lover, or swindle your friends. Or find inner peace.

But after one has negotiated, appreciated, and ingested the ins and outs of keeping pigeons, there are, considering the times—and you know what times we live in: whole libraries for sale, art books, leather-bound in Baghdad in the thirties, obstetrics and radiology texts, copies of *British Medical Journals*. And something for you as well: first and second editions of *The Sun Also Rises*. *Waiting for Godot*. And all for the price of a few cigarettes—considering the times there is only one real rule to keeping pigeons. And this rule, this golden rule is Not in this book: never name a pigeon after a member of your family or a dear friend. *(Beat)* For two reasons: pigeons have short lives—and when a pigeon named after an uncle dies, this can be disconcerting. And second. These times are dangerous for pigeons: they can be caught and eaten . . .

And cannibalism can put you off a hobby.

I began collecting and trading pigeons and doves when I was fifteen. That was more than ten years ago, when birds clustered like flies in the palms along the avenues and my land was the land of dates. Do you remember that country? Back then, everyone could read and when my smallest dove developed a fever, I took her to the hospital, where there was free access to all health care facilities. Parents were fined for not sending their pigeons to school. The basic indicators that you use to measure the overall well-being of flying animals were some of the best in the world. And. And. *(Gently but firmly to himself)* Shut up, Ali.

One of the birds I called Lak'aa Faseeh Zayer, after my grandmother. A real show-off, she was. This bird, known as a feral pigeon or rock dove, I bought off a trader from North America: *Columba livia*, in Latin. It has a white rump and a double black wing bar. Now my grandmother was tall and hard as a big stick and she liked everything American. She drank her coffee from a Campbell's Soup can. She worked as a maid in a hotel wearing a set of trainers from a Sears Roebuck catalogue a cousin sent her from Wisconsin. I was already a teenager when I got my first pigeon but when I had trouble sleeping she would hold me in her arms and sing to me. Her voice was like an old soft motor, clinking and clanking. Much sweeter than any fruit:

(He sings a short Arab lullaby his grandmother taught him.)

She had only three teeth in front but she always said song was not in the tooth but in the roof of the mouth, where God lives. She was also a bit of a blasphemer. Lak'aa Faseeh Zayer was her name. I would write her name down for you but we have no pencils.

I became a student when I was seventeen. I had six birds by then. I had one white-winged dove, also imported from America. She I named Greta, after my little sister. My father he loved movies and so my mother named my sister Greta, after Garbo. We were secular, our family. My birds, they were a mix of Christian, Jewish, and Muslim. They pulled out each other's feathers when they got a chance, sometimes even a little blood but mostly they got along well and crapped in the same pile. I won third prize with Greta in 1989 at the International Bird Show in Baghdad.

Books have other uses.

(He stands on the book.)

Now I am an inch and a half taller. *(He stands with one foot off and one foot on.)* Now I am a crooked man, a slanted man. Or to cut it short, for most of the world: an Arab. And I have come here to speak to you about pigeons:

My favorite bird is the *Zenaida macroura*, or mourning dove. Its name derives from its long, mournful, cooing call, which sounds something like this:

(He makes a very impressive call of the mourning dove.)

The mourning dove is a strong, fast flier that flushes up with a whirring of its wings. This first dove I bought, I named after my closest friend, Samir Saboura. We went to grade school together. While I drew birds, he made up words. He made up a word for the motion of a stone falling. *(Speaks a made-up word, with confidence)* The way a fish flicks its tail in the water. *(Another word)* The sound an apple makes when it's bit. *(Another word)* Samir Saboura. A strong fast flier that flushed up with a whirring of his wings.

My grandmother, Lak'aa Faseeh Zayer, took care of my pigeons when I was conscripted. Samir and I, we were in Saddam's army, not the elite Republican Guard, but just the ordinary shock troops. What luck. What luck that we managed to stay together throughout the war. We hid in bunkers for most of those weeks. Cursing Saddam when our captain was out. Cursing the Brits and the Yanks the rest of the time. And I missed my birds. But birds were prohibited in the bunkers. Prohibited. Prohibited by the laws of nations as were the fuel air explosive bombs, the napalm—Shhhh!—the cluster and antipersonnel weapons. Prohibited, as were the BLU-82 bombs, a fifteen thousand pound device—Shut up!—capable of incinerating every living thing, flying or grounded, within hundreds of yards . . . And me, I missed my birds. The way they looked at me, their eyes little pieces of peace sailing my way.

After the war, I sold them one by one, all twelve of them. For food. For aspirin. I sold them. But not before I sold the watch my great uncle gave me, the spoon my aunt gave mother, with my name inscribed the day I was born. Not before I sold my Shakespeare, in Arabic, first, then my copies in English. Because I knew. I knew. That my birds would not be shown at the next convention.

I remember. I remember. Everything we say these days begins with "I remember." Because the things we saved from the past, we sell day by day for a future in a bucket of slops and potato skins. A bunch of Dole bananas and a bag of apples from Beirut cost a teacher's salary for a month. Only the rich eat fruit. So all we can do is remember. I remember, a few months after the bombing stopped, my grandmother falling on a piece of broken pipe, her thigh cut to the bone. Little pink pills. Little pink pills of penicillin were all she needed. But these were prohibited by the blockade, prohibited for import, as are chemotherapy drugs and painkillers—Not again, Ali!—

(Beat) Five thousand pigeons die a month because of this blockade. No. *(Beat)* Five thousand children die a month because of this blockade . . . I will count to five thousand and then perhaps you will see how many five thousand is. *(Slowly)* One, two, three, four, five, six, seven, eight, nine, ten, eleven, twelve, thirteen, fourteen. *(Beat)* It takes a long time to count that far.

Little pink pills. That was all we needed to save Lak'aa Faseeh Zayer, my grandmother. She lay in my mother's arms, rotting from the waist down while the birds disappeared from the avenues because the trees had died. And this was the land of dates. How many dates? How many birds? *(Slowly)* One, two, three, four. The sadness of numbers is that they do not stop and there is always one more to follow. Just like birds.

(He quotes.)

"Do you ne'er think who made them, and who taught
The dialect they speak, where melodies
Alone are the interpreters of thought?"

"The Birds of Killingworth," Henry Wadsworth Longfellow. He was one of Samir's favorites, along with al-Sayyab, Kanafani, and Darwish. And of course, the poets of love. *(Beat)* And what of love? What is a book on the pigeon and the dove if it does not treat the philosophies of love? Is it in the young boy's kiss that smells like dust from the dove that has been flying for miles and miles with hunger a sharp blue light across its breast, coming home, coming home? Is it in the woman's spine, rolling up and down, dice from the fire? Is it in the child's sleep, where death is a butterfly that rests on the finger, then away? I don't know. *(Beat)* I don't know what love is. It goes. It comes. It goes. It comes. Samir Saboura. My friend. If love is in pieces, then he was a piece of love.

Tall, tall, he was. A handsome fellow with big dark eyes but, and I must say it, he walked like a pigeon. Now, pigeons are not really meant to walk. Their state of grace is to fly. But if they must walk, they walk like Samir walked. Like this:

(He walks like Samir, bobbing is head in and out, taking sure but awkward steps.)

It's possible his great grandfather was a flamingo. Samir. He was intelligent and hilarious, but he had one fault: he could hardly read. He was terribly dyslexic. So we would do the reading for him. Samir was always carrying a book, and whoever he came upon, he would say "Read to me." He'd memorize whole passages that he would recite at the most inopportune of moments. For instance, I had food poisoning when I was sixteen. All day I sat on the toilet, rocking and moaning. And, I must say it, stinking as well. But Samir would not leave my side. He would not leave me to suffer alone. Up and down the hallway outside the bathroom he strode, reciting pieces of Hart Crane. While I sputtered and farted in agony, snatches of *The Bridge* sailed in and out of my consciousness and kept me from despair:

(He quotes Samir reciting Hart Crane.)

"And if they take your sleep away sometimes
They give it back again. Soft sleeves of sound
attend the darkling harbour, the pillowed bay."

A good friend, Samir. He had a library that even his teachers envied. He couldn't read the books himself, but he slept and ate among them. Running his big hands over their spines, he would grin at us: "I cannot read them, but I can touch them." He was so intimate with his books that he could close his eyes and find a book by its smell.

(He tears a small piece of paper from a book and smells it, then eats it.)

Books can also, in extreme times, be used as sustenance. But such eating makes for a parched throat. Many mornings I wake and I am thirsty. I turn on the taps but there is no running water. A once-modern city of three million people, with no running water for years now. The toilets are dry because we have no sanitation. Sewage pools in the streets. When we wish to relieve ourselves, we squat beside the dogs. At night, we turn on the lights to read the books we have forgotten we have sold, but there is no electricity. We go to the cupboard to eat cold cans of soup but there is no food processing so the cupboards are bare. A couple of us wanted to write a few polite words of complaint to the United Nations Sanctions Committee, but it has blocked the import of pencils as it is feared they might be used for making "weapons of mass destruction." Just recently it was reported that despite the blockade, at the very tops of some of the most remote mosques, nests have been found made entirely of pencils. *(Whispers)* Stockpiling.

(He opens the book again.)

Sometimes, if the occasion is right, a book is for reading.

(He snaps the book shut then recites quietly.)

"Some say the world will end in fire,
Some say ice.
From what I've tasted of desire,
I hold with those who favor fire."

Robert Frost. You teach that in school. Eighty-eight thousand five hundred tons of bombs. Write this down without pencils: the equivalent of seven and a half atomic bombs of the size that incinerated Hiroshima. Nine hundred tons of radioactive waste spread over much of what was once the land of dates. *(He gets rid of the book.)* Somewhere within this information is a lullaby.

(Sings a piece of the Arab lullaby that he sang before. Beat)

And this, my friends, is documented. Fact. Fact. By the European Parliament, 1991. Members of the committee recorded the testimony, drinking cups of cold coffee: the defeated troops were surrendering. We, a nation of "unpeople," were surrendering. Samir and myself, alongside seven hundred other men. We were dirty and tired and hungry, sucking orange mints because the napalm made our gums bleed. That morning, I'd relieved myself beside the others while invisible jets broke the black glass sky across the horizon. My friend Samir did the same. And then we walked towards the American unit to surrender, our arms raised beside seven hundred other men. Samir, he said to me— this is not documented—He said: I want to put my hands in a bucket of cold water. Shut up, I said, keep your hands up. Samir said, I want to smell the back of my father's neck. Shut up, I said. Shut up. We're almost home. Samir Saboura said, "I want to tell an astonishing joke until you cry for relief."

As we walked towards them—this is documented—the commander of the US unit fired, at one man, an anti-tank missile. A missile meant to pierce armor. At one man. The rest of us, arms still raised, stopped walking. I remember. I remember. I could not. I could not recognize. My friend Samir. A piece of his spine stuck upright in the sand. His left hand blown so high in the air it was still falling. Then they opened fire on the rest of us.

A bullet hit me in the back as I ran. Out of hundreds, thousands in that week, a handful of us survived. I lived. *(Beat)* Funny. That I am still here. The dead are dead. The living, we are the ghosts. We no longer say goodbye to one another. With the pencils we do not have we write our names so the future will know we were here. So that the past will know we are coming.

(He quotes.)

"In a world that seems so very puzzling is it any wonder birds have such appeal? Birds are, perhaps, the most eloquent expression of reality."

Roger Tory Peterson, American ornithologist, born 1908. *(He quotes again.)*

"War is hell."

Pete Williams, Defense Department spokesman, on confirming that US Army earth movers buried alive, in their trenches, up to eight thousand Iraqi soldiers. *(Beat)* Yep. Yep. War is hell. And birds are perhaps the most eloquent expression of reality. In Arabic we say:

(Says in Arabic, twice, the equivalent of "fuck that.")

Which is the equivalent of: "fuck that."

I sold my last bird a few days ago. Tomorrow I will sell the cage. The day after that I will have nothing more to sell. But I keep track of the buyers, and who the buyers sell to. I go to their homes and I ask for the bones. Usually the family is kind, or frightened of me, and they give me the bones after the meal. I boil the bones and keep them in a bucket.

(We now notice an old steel bucket that is elsewhere on stage. He takes the bucket.)

Listen.

(He shakes the bucket. We hear the sound of bones rattling, though the sound comes not from his bucket but from all around us.)

It is a kind of music.

(He holds the bucket out to the audience.)

These are the bones of those who have died, from the avenue of palms, from the land of dates. I have come here to give them to you for safekeeping. *(Beat)* Catch them. If you can.

(He roughly throws the contents of the bucket at the audience. Instead of bones, into the air and across the audience spill hundreds of white feathers.)

The Perfect Dive

MIC WEINBLATT

A diver's last thoughts before making the most important dive of his life.

It is recommended that all diving boards be set up and maintained according to requirements especially with regard to elevation and pitch. The springboards shall be one meter and three meters above the water level. The front edge of the board shall project at least five feet and preferably six feet beyond the edge of the pool. All dives must be executed by the competitor, without assistance from any other person. In the event that the diver is injured during any of the competition and is unable to continue, the diver shall be disqualified. The four elements of the dive will be judged as described:

1. The approach,
2. The take off,
3. The technique and grace during the passage through the air, and
4. The entry into the water.

These thoughts churn and swirl in my brain as I stand on the edge of the precipice. The crowd cheers and the tension is palpable. Though I can't see my parents from up here, I know they're watching, that they're proud of their son, and that they've forgiven me for what I've done in the past. I can see the TV crews focused on me: ready to document the most significant dive of my life. It's important that my form be perfect and conforms to the regulations. I don't want the judges to take any points off because I didn't make enough twists or turns in the air or my back wasn't arched or I looked frightened or too resolute as I was about to make contact. I test the board and realize it doesn't have the spring or give I need. I compensate by stepping a little further out on the narrow board. I set my foot lightly on the end of it and mentally see my body arching, undulating and spinning in the air as I execute my dive. My feet are close together, my shoulders pushed back, my chest tucked under my chin, my body erect. I take several deep breaths and visualize my entry into the water. I can see my body breaking the surface like an arrow, without a splash. I can hear the screams, the hysteria, the frenzy of my fans as they urge me on and then stop awe-struck as they witness the perfect dive. Now is the time. I know my seven judges will be looking for flawless form and I mustn't disappoint them. Dear God, let this dive be forceful, reasonably confident, and proceed without undue delay Amen. I take two steps back so that I can get a running start to compensate for the inferior board and I run and explode into the air. There is a howl of encouragement quickly followed by a hushed, almost religious stillness as my fans watch me dive effortlessly from the fiftieth floor window of my apartment onto the smooth, wet, rain-soaked concrete.

Things to Lose

RANDY WYATT

MICHAEL is a male in his early thirties.

MICHAEL: I lose things.

I always have. I misplace my wallet on the bus. I forget my keys at home. I leave my day planner at every other restaurant.

Every paperback book I have ever been seriously interested in I've had to buy twice.

I keep my bus pass on a chain around my neck. Along with my driver's license. I cut up my credit cards. I laugh when salespeople offer me cell phones.

I lose my place, my sense of direction. I will come home hours and hours after lunch, the moon a hole gushing light over the lawn. Fortunately, I don't work, or I'd have lost my job long ago.

I try. I do. I endeavor to maintain some sort of schedule. I set my alarm every night with the best of intentions. The radio roars to life at 6:11 every morning. Country, I hate country. We both did.

I roll over to his side of the bed to avoid getting up on the wrong side. The radio keeps going long after I've left the room.

By the time I reach the shower, I've forgotten what the big deal was. I turn the handles and water and steam fall. I sit down cross-legged under the shower until I am shivering.

The house is silent. I pad downstairs half-dressed. The coffeemaker has started but I don't drink coffee. I just need the smell. It's not morning, it's not normal unless.

Mark made candy. He'd kiss me and rush out the door to the shop. He'd come home smelling of chocolate and pralines and raspberry creams. I'd lick them off his fingers and somehow never finish my 4:30 whiskey sour.

We're not like other couples, he'd tell me through a wolfish smile. We're staying together. He'd roll on top of me and I'd laugh until I'd feel his warm stare. I'm stuck with you, he'd say. I'm stuck with you.

I threw out a lot of things afterwards. Things. They lost their names.

I went to my landlord to ask if I could move into a one-bedroom. She gripped my hands and her tears were clear and beautiful. "I'm so sorry you've lost him," she said. I couldn't speak back to her, just beamed and nodded, squeezing her hand back, as if I were holding onto her kindness.

The next week there was broken glass on our living room floor. The television was missing, some other things. I picked up the telephone to call the police and froze. I sat down and stared at the shards of glass, like tea leaves at the bottom of my cup, telling my future. Take it, I thought with gratitude. Take it all away. I'll just lose it.

Mark died in winter. It took me all of spring to remember how to make a pot of tea. Day by day, I felt the satisfaction of a kid who knocked down his own sandcastle. Erasing our lives became the satisfaction of a deeper hunger than I knew I had.

I don't remember when the carelessness wasn't welcome anymore, but I heard a voice, like wrapped in cotton, deep in my chest, don't lose it all. Don't forget it all. And I remember crying helplessly to my friends, blubbering my request for help, please don't let me lose it all. And they understood, and they packed boxes and took them away, and even though I didn't know where they were exactly, I knew they were safe, secured under Gerome's bed, or in Hannah's office, or deep in my mother's hall closet.

Today I was offered a simple chocolate by a store clerk. Sure, I said. I closed my eyes in the dull pain of remembrance as I slipped it into my mouth. Why not? I said, my mouth and mind flooding with Friday afternoons and keepsake whispers, that which I could not box up.

Nothing to lose, I thought.

Contributors

Janet Allard's plays include *Incognito* (Guthrie Theater commission), *Loyal* (Guthrie and The Children's Theatre Company joint commission), *The Unknown: a silent musical* (Jonathan Larson Fellowship), and *Untold Crimes of Insomniacs* (developed in the Playwrights' Center's PlayLabs, a Guthrie/University of Minnesota BFA program 2004 Guthrie Lab premiere). Producing theaters include Mixed Blood, the Kennedy Center, Playwrights Horizons, Yale Rep, the Yale Cabaret, Access Theater in New York City, and theaters in Ireland, England, Greece, and New Zealand. Janet has received two Jerome Fellowships at the Playwrights' Center, where she is a core member. She holds an MFA from the Yale School of Drama.

Abi Basch is a 2004–2005 and 2005–2006 Jerome Fellow at the Playwrights' Center. Her Jerome-winning play, *Voices Underwater* was in the Bay Area Playwrights Festival and Theater Emory's Brave New Works Series and was a finalist for the Weissberger Award at Williamstown Theatre Festival. She works closely with Physical Plant Theater in Austin, Texas, and is a core member of Austin Script Works. In 2005 she will receive an MFA in playwriting from the University of Texas.

Alan M. Berks' plays have been seen at the Phoenix Theatre (Indianapolis), the Riverside Repertory (Albuquerque), Blackball Ensemble (Phoenix), and Strawdog Theatre (Chicago). He was a 2003–2004 Jerome Fellow at the Playwrights' Center and was a finalist for the Princess Grace Award. He has an MFA in creative writing with an emphasis in playwriting. Alan is also an actor and a director.

Anne Bertram's plays include *Liability* (2002 Tennessee Williams One-Act Prize winner), *St. Luke's* (1999 Studio Z commission, 2001 premiere, Theatre Unbound in Minneapolis), *The Donner Gold* (2000 Playwrights' Center Jones Commission), and *Sherry's Basement* (2003 premiere, Theatre Unbound). She is managing director of Theatre Unbound and an associate member of the Playwrights' Center.

Janea Rae Boyles studied at the John F. Kennedy Center and Kennesaw State University. Her plays have been produced at the Mae West Fest and the Seen and Heard Atlanta Women's Arts Festival. Readings of her work have been held through the Essential Theatre (Atlanta), the Mockingbird Theatre (Nashville), and the Last Frontier Theatre Conference. She was a finalist for a 2003–2004 Jerome Fellowship at the Playwrights' Center.

Richard Broadhurst has had plays produced in New York City, Los Angeles, and at the Sacramento Theatre Company (where he is a resident playwright and artist). He was commissioned by Stages Theatre (Hopkins, Minnesota) to write the play *Ritual*. In 2004 he was a guest playwright at the William Inge Theatre Festival (Independence, Kansas). In 2003 he participated in the Jungle Theater's new play reading series (Minneapolis). Richard also writes for film. Richard's *Requiem for a Woman's Soul* aired on NPR and was awarded outstanding radio drama of the year.

Carlyle Brown's plays include *The African Company Presents Richard III*, *The Little Tommy Parker Celebrated Colored Minstrel Show*, *The Negro of Peter the Great*, and others. "White Girl from the Projects" was developed in the Playwrights' Center's PlayLabs and premiered at the Pillsbury House Theatre as part of Carlyle's *Talking Masks*, coproduced by Carlyle Brown and Company, 2004. His commissions include Arena Stage, Houston Grand Opera, The Children's Theatre Company, Alabama Shakespeare Festival, and Actors Theatre of Louisville, which cocommissioned *Pure Confidence* which will premiere at the 2005 Humana Festival. Carlyle has received fellowships from the New York Foundation for the Arts, the Minnesota State Arts Board, the Rockefeller Foundation, the National Endowment for the Arts, Theatre Communications Group, the Pew Charitable Trust, and the McKnight and Jerome Foundations through the Playwrights' Center, where he is a core alumnus. He is also an alumnus of New Dramatists. Carlyle is currently on the board of directors of Theatre Communications Group.

Cory Busse is a playwright and humorist in Minneapolis. His play *Little Vines* was a semifinalist for the Playwrights' Center's 2003 PlayLabs Festival. In addition to plays and screenplays, Cory has written for *A Prairie Home Companion*, Salon.com, and PBS' *Mental Engineering*.

Sheila Callaghan's plays *Kate Crackernuts, Scab, We Are Not These Hands, The Hunger Waltz, The Catherine Calamity, Dead City,* and *Crawl Fade to White* have been produced or developed with the Playwrights' Center, ASK Theatre Projects, Playwright's Horizons, Soho Rep, Actors Theatre of Louisville, New Georges, Annex Theatre, LAByrinth, the Flea, and elsewhere. Her awards include the Princess Grace Award, a Chesley Prize for Lesbian Playwriting, a MacDowell Fellowship, a Playwrights' Center Jerome Fellowship, and commissions from EST/Sloan Foundation and South Coast Repertory.

Beth Cleary's *Findings Uncertain: A Play about Adoption in Three Pieces* was included in the June 2003 Theatre Unbound Festival of New Play Readings at Boston Theatreworks. The play received its first reading at the Playwrights' Center, as did her other short plays, *Break* and *Dialectical Soup. Break* was published in the fall 2003 issue of *Cross-Cultural Poetics.* She directs and teaches theater at Macalester College in St. Paul, Minnesota.

Bill Corbett's plays include *The Big Slam, Hate Mail* (cowritten with Kira Obolensky), *Heckler,* and *Ridiculous Dreaming,* an adaptation of Heinrich Boll's *The Clown.* He recently wrote *The Stuff of Dreams,* a Guthrie Theater touring production. His plays have been produced by Primary Stages (New York), Woolly Mammoth (Washington, D.C.), A Contemporary Theater (Seattle), and many other theaters. He was also a writer and performer for TV's *Mystery Science Theater 3000.*

Jeannine Coulombe has written several full-length plays, which have been produced in Minnesota and Iowa. Her play *The Vacant Lot* won the National AIDS Fund CFDA-Vogue Initiative Award for Playwriting from the Kennedy Center in 2001. She is an artistic associate with Theatre Unbound (Minneapolis). She has been a member of the Playwrights' Center since 1997. She received an MFA from the Playwrights Workshop at the University of Iowa in 2003.

Stephen J. Cribari is a poet and playwright whose work includes *Listening to Mozart* (Works/Plays, Minneapolis, 2003) and *Sonata for Solo Cello* (SummerPlay '99, Denver). He is colibrettist of the peace oratorio *Where Are We Now?* (Germany, 2000). His poem *On Bernini's Statue of Daphne and Apollo* was published in connection with the dance oratorio *Bernini* (Germany, 2003). His poem *Adagio for Violin* is scored for voice, violin, and piano.

Stephen R. Culp is the author of *The 13 Hallucinations of Julio Rivera, Life on Pluto, The Fool Jumps, Let's All Clap, Decadent Lawyers in Heat, Gods in Relief, Kitty,* and *The End of the World and Every Day After.* His work has been produced at the Magic Theatre in San Francisco, the Lark Theatre in New York, Manhattan Class Company, and the Organic Theater in Chicago, among others. He happily boasts that he's a descendant of Mark Twain, and he's a member of the Dramatists Guild.

Vincent Delaney's plays include *The Robeson Tape, The War Party, MLK and the FBI,* and *Kuwait.* His plays have been seen at the Humana Festival of New Plays, the Alabama Shakespeare Festival, Woolly Mammoth, the Empty Space Theatre, A Contemporary Theatre, the Illusion Theatre, and the Cleveland Play House. Vince is a core member and 2004–2005 McKnight Advancement Grant recipient at the Playwrights' Center, and a former Bush Foundation Artist Fellow. He holds an MFA in playwriting from the University of California–Davis.

Matt Di Cintio is a playwright, translator, and freelance dramaturg. His productions include a translation of Wilde's *Salome* (PlayMakers Repertory, 2003), an adaptation of *Moby-Dick* (University of Richmond, 2003), *Nosegays on Monday* (Glasslight, 2003), and *The Valets* (Outward Spiral/Minnesota Fringe Festival, 2004), with dramaturgy at PlayMakers Rep, the Guthrie Theater, TheatreVirginia, and the University of Richmond. He holds an MA in romance languages from the University of North Carolina and BAs in theater and French from the University of Richmond. He has received W. M. Keck grants for playwriting and translation.

Matthew A. Everett holds an MFA from the Yale School of Drama. He is the recipient of a Drama-Logue Award (*Heaven and Home*) and a Minnesota State Arts Board Theater Fellowship (*The Surface of the World*) and Career Opportunity Grant (*The Hopes and Fears of All the Years*). Further monologues, scenes, and information on his plays are available at *www.matthewaeverett.com.*

Diane Glancy is a professor at Macalester College in St. Paul, Minnesota. She has published two collections of plays, *American Gypsy* and *War Cries.* Among her productions are *Jump Kiss,* in Native Voices at the Autry in Los Angeles (2002); *Lesser Wars,* Voice & Vision Theater Company in New York (1999); and *The Woman Who Was a Red Deer Dressed for the Deer Dance* and *The Women Who Loved House Trailers,* Raw Space, Sage Theater Company in New York (1998–99).

Daphne Greaves is a recent graduate of the playwriting program at the Juilliard School and the winner of the 2004 National Graduate Playwriting Competition. Her historical drama, *Day of the Kings,* received its world premiere performance at the Alliance Theater in January 2005. It will be published by Broadway Play Publishing in the forthcoming Lark Center for Play Development's anthology of new plays. Her other plays include *Killing Time, Shade,* and *Crash!*

Irving A. Greenfield is seventy-six years old and has written and had published many novels and short stories. Irving has been married to his wife for fifty-four years. His two sons are also authors. He taught at Wagner College in Staten Island for eighteen years and is still a research fellow there.

Native New Yorker **June Guralnick** is the author of nine full-length plays and various shorts performed at venues including the Kennedy Center, the Henry Street Settlement Experimental Theatre (New York), the Southern Appalachian Repertory Theatre (Mars Hill, North Carolina), and the North Carolina Museum of Art. She has received a National Endowment for the Arts grant and a North Carolina Arts Council Literature Fellowship; additionally, she has been a Pinter Drama Review Prize silver medalist, a Southern Appalachian Repertory Theatre's National New Plays contest winner, and a Mid-Atlantic Arts Foundation's America Creates for the Millennium finalist. Visit *www.juneguralnick.com* for additional information.

Jordan Harrison's plays have been produced and developed at Actors Theatre of Louisville, Perishable Theatre, the Empty Space Theatre, Playwrights Horizons, Clubbed Thumb, and the Playwrights' Center's PlayLabs. He is the recipient of the Heideman Award, two Jerome Fellowships from the Playwrights' Center, and a Lucille Lortel Fellowship. He is currently working on a commission from The Children's Theatre Company and the Guthrie Theater. Jordan coedits the annual *Play: A Journal of Plays.*

Jeffrey Hatcher's plays have been produced on Broadway, Off-Broadway, and at numerous theaters in the United States and abroad. In addition to the American Theatre Critics Association Award and Philadelphia's Barrymore Award for Best New Play, he's received fellowships and awards from the Playwrights' Center's McKnight and Jerome programs, the Charles MacArthur Foundation, the National Endowment for the Arts, Theatre Communications Group, and the

Lila Wallace-Readers' Digest Fund. He is a member of the Dramatists Guild and the Writers Guild of America as well as a Playwrights' Center core alumnus and a New Dramatists alumnus.

Ryan Hill, a multidisciplinary theater artist, has had his work produced in New York, Berlin, Beijing, and the Twin Cities. A playwright, performer, and director, he's passionate about exploring the form and context of dramatic text. He is a Fulbright Scholar and has performed and studied with director Robert Wilson. Born and raised in northern Wisconsin, Ryan has lived in Berlin and New York; he currently resides in Minneapolis. His first published work, *The Ferry,* is available from Samuel French.

Cory Hinkle is a playwright and actor from Bartlesville, Oklahoma. He received his BFA in performance from the University of Oklahoma. He is the recipient of a 2003–2004 Jerome Fellowship at the Playwrights' Center as well as a new play commission from the Guthrie Theater. His plays include *Unrequited Pop, The Magazine Girl, Across the Desert, Sex and Cigarettes,* and *Kid Dreams.* He has been a runner-up for the Princess Grace Award and a semifinalist for the Playwrights' Center's PlayLabs.

Award-winning playwright **Mark Steven Jensen** is a core member of the Playwrights' Center. His plays include *Independency, Atomic Summer, Runestone, The Benevolent Women's Craft Society,* and *A Chat with Him and Her.* He was the 2003 Playwright-in-Residence at the Utah Shakespearean Festival. Hollywood Playhouse will produce the world premiere of *A Chat with Him and Her* in May 2005.

Minnesotan **Kevin Kling** has a BA in theater from Gustavus Adolphus College. His productions and solo performance tours here and abroad include *Fear and Loving in Minneapolis, 21A, Lilly's Purple Plastic Purse, Home and Away, Lloyd's Prayer* (workshopped at the Sundance Institute), *From the Charred Underbelly of the Yule Log* (Guthrie Theater), and others. Kevin contributes to NPR's *All Things Considered* and has produced four CDs of his commentaries. In 2004, *At Your Service* was produced by Ten Thousand Things Theater Company (Minneapolis) and *Whoppers* was in the Minnesota Fringe Festival and toured England. Kevin recently received a Bush Playwriting Fellowship from the Guthrie Theater.

Carson Kreitzer's plays include *The Love Song of J. Robert Oppenheimer, Slither, Self Defense or death of some salesmen,* and *Take My Breath*

Away, among others. She is a member of the Dramatists Guild and an associate member of the Playwrights' Center. She has received grants from the New York Foundation for the Arts, the New York State Council on the Arts, the National Endowment for the Arts, and Theatre Communications Group. She has also received two Jerome Fellowships and a McKnight Advancement Grant through the Playwrights' Center. She currently lives in Austin, Texas.

Katie Leo is an adopted Korean actor, writer, and educator in the Twin Cities. Her essays have been published in *Journal of the Asian American Renaissance* and *HardKore Magazine.* Her poetry has been heard at Passions Spoken Word Night, People's Open Mic, and Hotbed, as well as the upcoming Revolutionary Women Series. She is a core member of MaMa mOsAiC, a women of color theater collective, for whom she cowrites scripts dealing with issues affecting all women.

Patricia Lynch is a two-time Playwrights' Center Jerome Playwriting Fellow, winner of the Kennedy Center's Fund for New American Plays Roger L. Stevens Award, and a Theatre Communications Group artist fellowship recipient as well as the recipient of other awards. Her plays have been produced by The Children's Theatre Company, Stage Left Theatre, First Stage, Illusion Theater, the Great American History Theater, 7 Stages, Horizon Theatre, Stages, and Brass Tacks Theatre. Her works have been included in national development conferences and workshopped in theaters around the country. She is a core alumnus of the Playwrights' Center.

Jennifer Maisel's plays include *The Last Seder, Eden, Dark Hours, Mad Love, . . . And the Two Romeos,* and *Mallbaby,* which was developed at the Playwrights' Center's PlayLabs and ASK Theatre Projects. Her plays have been workshopped and produced in New York, Chicago, Washington, D.C., Minneapolis, San Francisco, and Los Angeles. Awards include the Roger L. Stevens Award (*Mad Love*) and the Charlotte Woolard award for most promising new writer, and the Fund for New American Plays award from the Kennedy Center (*The Last Seder*). In addition, she was a winner of the California Playwrights Competition (*Eden*) and a finalist for the PEN West Literary Award (*Mad Love*) and the Heideman Award (*How I Learned to Spell*).

Allison Moore is a displaced Texan living in Minneapolis, where she is a two-time Jerome Fellow and former McKnight Advancement Grant recipient at the Playwrights' Center. Her plays include *Eighteen, Urgent*

Fury, CowTown, Hazard County, and *The Strange Misadventures of Patty.* . . . She has received commissions from the Guthrie Theater, Eye of the Storm, and Actors Theatre of Louisville; and her work has been developed or produced at the O'Neill Playwrights Conference, Kitchen Dog Theater, InterAct Theatre Company, Madison Rep, Centenary Stage Company, the Jungle Theater, the Playwright's Center, and the Humana Festival. Allison is a graduate of Southern Methodist University and holds an MFA from the Iowa Playwrights Workshop.

Kira Obolensky's play *Quick Silver* (developed in PlayLabs and coproduced by 3Legged Race and the Playwrights' Center) was named most outstanding piece of experimental theater by Twin Cities critics in 2003. Her other plays include *Lobster Alice* (Kesselring Prize; finalist for Susan Smith Blackburn; published in *Best Plays by American Women 2000*; and produced in Minneapolis, Atlanta, California, Texas, and Off-Broadway) and *The Adventures of Herculina* (Honorable Mention Kesselring Prize, Edith Oliver Award, produced in Chicago and Minneapolis). Kira's new work includes *All Is Well in the Kingdom of Nice* (produced at Geva Theatre Center), *Hiding in the Open* (produced at the Great American History Theatre), and *A New House,* or *21 Lies for Four Characters.* She has received the Guggenheim Fellowship, the Bush Fellowship, and the Playwrights' Center Jerome Fellowship and is a current recipient of a Playwrights' Center McKnight Advancement Grant.

Dominic Orlando was a 2003–2004 Jerome Fellow at the Playwrights' Center, where he completed *Juan Gelion Dances for The Sun,* which was featured in the 2004 Bay Area Playwrights Festival in San Francisco. The play was developed at the MacDowell Colony in New Hampshire; the Edward Albee Foundation in Montauk, New York; and No-Pants Theatre through a grant from the New York City Department of Cultural Affairs. Dominic has also received commissions and fellowships from the Guthrie Theater, Nautilus Music Theater (St. Paul, Minnesota), Bristol Valley Theater (Naples, New York), the Cornucopia Arts Center (Lanesboro, Minnesota), and a second fellowship to the MacDowell Colony.

Daniel Pinkerton holds an MFA in playwriting and an MA in European history. A core member of the Playwrights' Center, he has been awarded a National Endowment for the Arts Music Theatre Fellowship, a Playwrights' Center Jerome Fellowship, and a Minnesota State

Arts Board Fellowship. His work has been seen at Red Eye Theater, the Jungle Theater, Nautilus Music Theater, Theater Latté Da, and Portland Stage Company's Little Festival of the Unexpected.

Mark Rosenwinkel is a core member of the Playwrights' Center, where he has received a Jerome Fellowship. His plays have had productions, readings, and workshops with theaters around the country, including the Idaho Shakespeare Festival and the Asolo Theatre (Sarasota, Florida). His four-person adaptation of *Moby-Dick* has been published by Dramatic Publishing, and his most recent play, *Sanctus*, won the 2002 Writers' Digest Literary Award in the play script category.

Gwendolyn Schwinke's plays have been produced by Red Eye Collaboration and Cheap Theatre in Minneapolis and read at the Playwrights' Center and the Cherry Lane Theatre in New York. A monologue from her play *Thrown by Angels* is included in Heinemann's *Even More Monologues for Women by Women* (2001). Gwendolyn is a core member of the Playwrights' Center and a past recipient of the center's Jones Commission.

Buffy Sedlachek is a resident artist with Stages Theatre Company and literary manager of the Jungle Theater. A core alumnus of the Playwrights' Center, she has been awarded Minnesota State Arts Board Fellowships, Playwrights' Center McKnight Advancement Grants and Jones Commissions, a Jerome Foundation Travel and Study Grant, and a Theatre Communications Group Observership. Nominated three times for the Susan Smith Blackburn Prize for distinguished women playwrights, she is also the coauthor of two curriculum guides for teaching playwriting.

Rosanna Staffa's work has been seen at the Mark Taper Forum's Taper, Too and the Odyssey Theatre Company in Los Angeles, Soho Rep and Off-Broadway in New York, and the Theatre Garage and the Playwrights' Center in Minneapolis. She has received new play commissions from the Guthrie Theater and The Children's Theatre Company. She is the recipient of an AT&T OnStage Award as well as a McKnight Advancement Grant and a Jerome Fellowship at the Playwrights' Center, where she is a core member.

Allan Staples' plays have been produced as part of the Minnesota Fringe Festival and the Jungle Theater's In the Spotlight Series. He is a member of Actors' Equity. He has stage-managed at the Fringe Festival, the Playwrights' Center, Frank Theatre, and the Jungle Theater, where he is the assistant to the producer.

Caridad Svich is a playwright, songwriter, translator, and editor. Her awards include a Harvard University Radcliffe Institute for Advanced Study Fellowship and a Theatre Communications Group/Pew National Theatre Artist Grant. Recent premieres include *Iphigenia . . . a rave fable* at 7 Stages (Atlanta) and her multimedia collaboration with Todd Cerveris and Nick Philippou, *The Booth Variations*, in New York. She is editor of *Trans-global Readings: Crossing Theatrical Boundaries* (MUP/Palgrave, 2004). She holds an MFA from University of California–San Diego and is a resident playwright of New Dramatists.

Naomi Wallace's plays have been produced at venues including Actors Theatre of Louisville's Humana Festival, Pittsburgh Public Theater, Long Wharf, the Royal Shakespeare Company and the Comedy Theatre in London's West End, and theaters in Athens' West End. *The Retreating World* was produced at the Latchmere Theatre (London) and throughout Europe in 2003. It will be published in *American Theatre's* one hundredth anniversary issue. Naomi has received the prestigious MacArthur Fellowship, the Susan Smith Blackburn Prize, the Fellowship of Southern Writers Drama Award, the Kesselring Prize, and the 1997 Obie award for the best play. She has received grants from the Kentucky Foundation for Women, the Kentucky Arts Council, and others.

Mic Weinblatt has been an actor, director, and writer in the Twin Cities for twenty years. His plays have been performed locally, in Chicago, and in California. He is a frequent contributor as a writer and an actor at the Playwrights' Center General Members' Roundtable and Ten-Minute Play Festival.

Randy Wyatt is an award-winning playwright, director, and improv coach. His plays include *The Face of the Earth* (a finalist in Christians in Theatre Arts 1999 playwriting competition), *Anticipating Miles* (in the 2004 Columbus GLBT Theatre Festival), and *32 Awkward Silences* (in the 2003 Austin Script Works Out of Ink Festival), *Saturday Morning Forever*, and *Sonata Blue*. He lives in Grand Rapids, Michigan; Minneapolis, Minnesota; or Austin, Texas, depending on where his current project is located.

Performance Rights

Janet Allard, c/o Doug Rand at Playscripts, Inc., P.O. Box 237060, New York, NY 10023; ph.: 866-639-7529 ext. 82; fax: 866-639-7529; drand@playscripts.com.
Abi Basch, c/o The Playwrights' Center, 2301 Franklin Ave. East, Minneapolis, MN 55406; ph: 612-332-7486.
Alan Berks, c/o Heinemann.
Anne Bertram, c/o Heinemann.
Janea Rae Boyles, c/o Heinemann.
Richard Broadhurst, c/o Heinemann.
Carlyle Brown, c/o Heinemann.
Cory Busse, c/o Heinemann.
Sheila Callaghan, c/o Heinemann.
Beth Cleary, c/o Heinemann.
Bill Corbett, c/o Carl Graham at Graham Agency, 311 West 43rd St., New York, NY 10036; grahamacnyc@aol.com.
Jeannine Coulombe, c/o Heinemann.
Stephen R. Culp, c/o Bruce Ostler at Bret Adams Ltd., 448 W. 44th St., New York, NY 10036; ph: 212-765-5630; fax: 212-265-2212; bostler.bal@verizon.net.
Vincent Delaney, c/o Heinemann.
Matt Di Cintio, c/o Heinemann.
Matthew A. Everett, c/o Heinemann.
Diane Glancy, c/o Heinemann.
Daphne Greaves, c/o Heinemann.
Irving Greenfield, c/o Heinemann.
June Guralnick, c/o Heinemann.
Jordan Harrison, c/o Val Day at William Morris Agency, 1325 Avenue of the Americas, New York, NY 10019; ph: 212-903-1550; pfasst@wma.com.

Jeffrey Hatcher, c/o William Morris Agency, 1325 Avenue of the Americas, New York, NY 10019; ph: 212-903-1125.

Ryan Hill, c/o Heinemann.

Cory Hinkle, c/o Heinemann.

Mark Steven Jensen, c/o Heinemann.

Kevin Kling, c/o Heinemann.

Carson Kreitzer, c/o cskreitzer@earthlink.net or Judy Boals at Judy Boals, Inc., 208 W. 30th St. #401, New York, NY 10001; ph: 212-868-0924; fax: 212-868-1052; jboals@earthlink.net.

Katie Leo, c/o Heinemann.

Patricia Lynch, c/o Heinemann.

Jennifer Maisel, c/o Susan Schulman, Agent, 454 West 44th St., New York, NY 10036; ph: 212-713-1633; fax: 212-581-8830; schulman@aol.com.

Allison Moore, c/o Maura Teitelbaum, Abrams Artist Agency, 275 7th Ave., 26th Floor, New York, NY 10001; ph: 646-486-4600; fax: 646-486-0100; maura.teitelbaum@abramsart.com.

Kira Obolensky, c/o Patrick Herold at ICM, 40 W. 57th St. 16th Floor, New York, NY 10019; ph: 212-556-5600; pherold@icmtalent.com.

Dominic Orlando, c/o Heinemann.

Daniel Pinkerson, c/o Heinemann.

Mark Rosenwinkel, c/o Heinemann.

Gwendolyn Schwinke, c/o Heinemann.

Buffy Sedlachek, c/o Heinemann.

Rosanna Staffa, c/o Susan Gurman, The Susan Gurman Agency, LLC., 865 West End Avenue, Suite 15A, New York, NY 10025; ph: 212-749-4618.

Alan Staples, c/o Heinemann.

Caridad Svich, c/o New Dramatists, 424 West 44th St., New York, NY 10036; ph: 212-886-1814 or 212-757-6960; fax: 212-265-4738; newdramatists@newdramatists.org.

Naomi Wallace, c/o Broadway Play Publishing, 56 E. 81st St., New York, NY 10028-0202; ph: 212-772-8334; www.broadwayplaypubl.com.

Mic Weinblatt, c/o Heinemann.

Randy Wyatt, c/o thecove@gmail.com or www.lostinthecove.com.